What people are saying about...

MIRROR OF TRUTH

Courage is doing what needs to be done when it needs to be done no matter the consequences. Esther had it and you can develop it through Christie's book: Act on Your Awareness.

Steve Arterburn, author, speaker, counselor,
host of #1 Christian radio talk-show New Life Live,
founder of New Life Ministries and Women of Faith

As both a social researcher and the mother of a teenage daughter, I am thrilled to find this Bible study that helps young women understand and apply God's deep and meaningful truths to their own unique, special lives. This will help launch a generation of young women into a deeper relationship with God, and into a willingness to allow Him to use their entire life to His glory!

Shaunti Feldhahn, best-selling author of For Women Only and
The Life Ready Woman Bible Study

Christie Rayburn knows Scripture and she knows young women, and she knows how to use the former to richly bless, challenge and encourage the latter. This study emphasizes just the right truths to help young women journey from feeling like defeated victims to becoming 'more than conquerors' in Christ Jesus.

Gary Thomas, Author of Sacred Marriage and
The Sacred Search

Danger - this Bible Study is not for those looking to check off a box on their spiritual "to do" list. It is for those with the hunger to go further - to look deeper - and find Jesus there waiting.
"Mirror of Truth" invites young women to walk with the confidence and graciousness that comes from walking with your hand in God's. It's practical, insightful and ready to rock your world.

Iona Snair, YFC, Associate Director of Lifeteams:
School of Youth Outreach,
college instructor, mentor and speaker

Christie hits the absolute core issues for a young woman in Mirror of Truth. This is part excellent Bible study and part incredible life coaching. I'm anxious to hand this resource to my 20 something daughters.

Jim Burns, PhD, President of HomeWord/Azusa Pacific University, Author of Confident Parenting and Getting Ready for Marriage

Mirror of Truth is a sensational "goldmine" when it comes to getting Godly nuggets that will enrich your life. Young women will eat up Christie's powerful and practical message. This study will end up being a classic.

Dr. Dave Currie, Ph.D., President of Doing Family Right, Executive Producer of TV show Marriage Uncensored with Dave & Christie

Christie Rayburn is passionate about helping young women view themselves through the lens of Biblical truth. Her commitment doesn't stop with explaining what the Bible says. Christie presses for application. This study promises to be a tool that leads to transformation.

Michael B. Pawelke, DMin, President of Briercrest College and Seminary

The Mirror of Truth is a unique blend of God's Word and Christie's wealth of experience, written in the exciting and dynamic tone of her exuberant spirit. Every young woman will grow from engaging in this study and learning from Christie's example.

John Van Epp, Ph.D., author of How To Avoid Marrying A Jerk, founder of Love Thinks, LLC

Mirrors: they can be a curse or a blessing. Look in one with the wrong perspective and you'll see something imperfect and lacking--you! Look in God's mirror and you'll gain the perfect perspective on life and yourself. You're in a critical season of your life. This book will help you look into the right mirror so you can reflect God's joy for you. Dive in!

Ron L. Deal, bestselling author of The Smart Stepfamily

MIRROR OF TRUTH

Becoming a Woman Who Is Confident,
Free, and a Powerful Influence

CHRISTIE RAYBURN

WESTBOW°
PRESS
A DIVISION OF THOMAS NELSON
& ZONDERVAN

Unless otherwise noted, Scripture quotations are from the Holy Bible, NEW INTERNATIONAL VERSION®, NIV® Copyright © 1973, 1978, 1984, 2011 by Biblica, Inc.® Used by permission. All rights reserved worldwide. Scripture quotations identified by the MSG are from THE MESSAGE © 1993, 1994, 1995, 1996, 2000, 2001, 2002. Used by permission of NavPress Publishing Group. Scripture quotations identified NASB are from the NEW AMERICAN STANDARD BIBLE®, © 1960, 1962, 1963, 1968, 1971, 1972, 1973, 1975, 1977,1995 by The Lockman Foundation. Used by permission. Scripture quotations identified NLT are from the Holy Bible, New Living Translation, copyright © 1996, 2004, 2007 by Tyndale House Foundation. Used by permission of Tyndale House Publishers, Inc., Carol Stream, Illinois 60188. All rights reserved.

WestBow Press books may be ordered through booksellers or by contacting:

WestBow Press
A Division of Thomas Nelson & Zondervan
1663 Liberty Drive
Bloomington, IN 47403
www.westbowpress.com
1 (866) 928-1240

Because of the dynamic nature of the Internet, any web addresses or links contained in this book may have changed since publication and may no longer be valid. The views expressed in this work are solely those of the author and do not necessarily reflect the views of the publisher, and the publisher hereby disclaims any responsibility for them.

Any people depicted in stock imagery provided by Thinkstock are models, and such images are being used for illustrative purposes only. Certain stock imagery © Thinkstock.

ISBN: 978-1-4908-9085-2 (sc)
ISBN: 978-1-4908-9086-9 (e)

Print information available on the last page.

WestBow Press rev. date: 10/01/2015

Dedicated to an answered prayer, my only daughter,

TAYLOR HOPE

From the moment you were born, I longed for a "heart touching heart" kind of relationship with you. Once again, my God has done exceedingly beyond anything I could have imagined or asked...He gifted me with the priceless treasure of a mother-daughter relationship where "soul touches soul."

Seated on the corner of my desk in a crystal frame, your beautiful, smiling face has been my inspiration. Every time I was stuck or wanted to give up, I would just look into your blue eyes imagining what I'd want to say to you. I would be reminded of how incredibly valuable it would be for you to know these Truths...then the keys would fly.

Never stop taking your soul to His Mirror of Truth and processing every nook and cranny of your heart through it. Always keep growing, sweetheart. Always keep falling in love with Jesus. All for His Glory.

There are no words big enough to express the joy you bring to my life or the love I have for you,

Momma

THANKFULLY ACKNOWLEDGING SO MANY...

GOD, FIRST & FOREMOST -- He is my everything, absolutely everything to me and everything for me; He called me, entrusted this to me, lead the way, provided every word and thought, exhibited endless patience, and gave me the courage; may He alone be glorified

MARK -- the biggest cheerleader in my life, his unconditional love for me is my tangible picture of Jesus

TAYLOR -- my personal assistant, editor and soundboard, my daughter overflowing with encouragement, support, and love

HUNTER AND COLTON -- my incredible sons who somehow think Mom can do anything

MIKE, IONA, and MYRNA -- hearts that gave of themselves to edit this study from their expertise and educated backgrounds

AMBER -- a generous sister who spent hours editing this study and turning my messes into something readable, one who went the extra mile

AMY -- a photographer extraordinaire who shared her incredible gift of art on behalf of sharing truth for young women

GRACE AND JESSICA -- servants who gave of their time over and over again

DARLENE and JEANNE -- Mirror Mirror's board members who advised and guided me with wisdom

PAM, ERYN-FAYE, SHELLEY, SHEILA -- friends who have walked before me as authors and gave insight

JILL and MARLA -- sisters who gave discernment, suggestions, and constant love

SUE, KAREN, MARY, JOANNE, LINDA (L3) -- the group of women I've met with monthly for over 17 years; they have covered every part of this study in prayer

WENDY, NANCY, MELINDA, GLORIA, LAURA, and ADRIAN-- friends who make a difference in my life with their prayer and encouraging support

MOM, JOANNE, AUNT LINDA, JEN, and JESS -- the priceless women in my family who have always believed in me

ADISON, KENNEDY, RILEY, ELLA, and BREELIN -- my beautiful nieces, how I pray that you would be women who look into the Mirror of Truth and have your hearts transformed

I am humbled and indebted. Thank you.

All photography by Amy R. Ballard of Amy B Photography, 2013.

Dear Amazing Young Woman, who has more potential than you could ever imagine,

I am writing this study FOR YOU--with a deep belief and even deeper hope that God will use this time to enable you to start looking in the mirror and grasping how beneficial it is for your life and your heart to do so purposefully.

We live in an emotionally and spiritually immature culture wherein we fill our lives with busyness. When there is a gap or void in our soul, we fill it with more activity instead of getting to the bottom of our issues. If we do come to the Mirror of Truth, God's holy and inspired Word, we find it easier to just read it or even study it versus seeking its wisdom for our own heart's transformation.

I long for His Spirit to call you to come away from the noise and busyness of this culture in order to look into the Mirror of Truth. Then ask yourself the tough questions and process your issues through this Truth, leading to a real change of heart.

If that happens, you will never be the same. As a result of taking the time and courage to look in the Mirror, you can actually become a confident young woman who doesn't battle insecurity on an hourly basis. You can live a life of freedom, not chained to your past or your fears or your strongholds. You can be a woman who turns this world upside down for Jesus Christ by becoming a powerful influence using her God-given voice, gifts, and passions. But it all starts with being willing to look into the mirror--His Mirror.

Dear one, God created you for big things and this world needs you at your maximum potential.

Let's get started by looking into the Mirror together, Christie Lee Rayburn

About This Study

Dear one, are you ready to be mentored by His truth for a season? Ready to look into His Mirror? Are you anticipating the change you will see when you look into your own mirror? It will most likely feel intense, like somebody has lit a fire under your feet, but the gold that will come out of it is sure to be priceless. I know it will be a challenge, but I believe that you are up for it.

You can do this study in two ways: (1) You can choose six weeks of commitment, which will consist of setting time aside to do five days of in-depth homework each week. (2) You can choose ten weeks of commitment, which will consist of setting time aside to do three days of in-depth homework each week. Whichever choice you make, it is best to meet in a small group with other Christ-followers once a week, in order to share with others what God is teaching you, support each other through prayer, and keep one another accountable to this commitment. Besides, growing within community is so much more fun!

I shared in my letter to you that I believe looking into the Mirror of Truth is critical to your growth and your ability to find satisfaction in Christ Jesus alone. However you can't just bring your mind to His Word. You need to bring your emotions, concerns, hurts, anxieties, fears, confusion, plans, and dreams to the Scriptures each day as you engage with your Lord in this precious dialogue. To help you learn how to do this, I've added these four components to practice each day.

STOP -- Within this culture of multi-tasking and instant gratification, you easily find yourself uncomfortable with the quiet of stillness. Yet, this is the fertile ground for intimacy to grow, and your soul craves intimacy with your Creator. So, follow the example of Jesus and come away from the noise of your life--the technology, the activity and busyness--so that you have the opportunity to hear your Father's voice clearly without distractions. See this time as your own mini-retreat each day. Abba Father eagerly anticipates spending one-on-one time with you.

LOOK -- There is only one absolute truth and only one place to look for it--the Bible. There is also only one person responsible for looking into it and one person responsible for knowing the Truth--you! But you shouldn't know it just for the sake of knowing it. God wants you to bring your heart and your soul to His truth so you can sift your life through it. His perfect wisdom is available to heal you, guide you, convict you, grow you, strengthen you, teach you, revive you, anchor you...and so much more. Don't miss out!

ASK -- Once you have looked into God's Word, then you have the opportunity to learn more about who God is and more about who you are. This is your chance to ask the real questions, the ones you tend to run from. God is big enough for any question, and He wants to reveal Himself to those who are seeking His heart. What are the parts of your soul that you keep running away from? Here is your chance to face yourself in His Mirror.

CHANGE -- In light of what has been revealed, it's then time to ask "What needs to change?" Here is the most critical step in this practice, yet the part that is most prominently skipped. You are not given revelation for the sake of instruction, but for the sake of transformation. Now that God has examined your heart, it's time to respond: "What attitude needs to radically change and how will you do that? What has been neglected and how will you begin to address it? What behavior needs to stop and how will you replace it?" The change in your life will always be about "the What" and "the How."

Sweet sister, if you keep doing what you've always done, I guarantee that you'll keep getting what you have always gotten. Authentic change is a process, not a shortcut. It's a process that involves time, truth, and effort. It begins with a deep desire that declares, "I want to change. This is important to me." Then it demands the power of both the Holy Spirit and the living Word of God.

You are about to set time aside for transformation--studying and digging into truth three or five days a week for the next six or ten weeks. May this effort bring you your heart's desire of connecting with God in an incredibly new way. May it impact your relationship with Him to such an extent that you practice this framework every time you go to God's Word for the rest of your life's journey.

STOP   LOOK   ASK   CHANGE

Starting Your First Week of Study

Our youngest child is now in driver's training... where has the time gone? As he practices driving in his momma's car, I keep reminding him about the blind spots. You can't drive safely if you aren't aware that you have blind spots in every vehicle. It's your job to discover where they are at and make the necessary adjustments.

Similarly, we as women have blind spots in our identity and character. If we continue to live with our blind spots, then we will always feel insecure and hesitant about our lives and our relationships. Whereas, awareness of ourselves exposes our blind spots. Addressing those blind spots breeds confidence. This confidence gives us the courage to grow as a person and address even more areas in order to drive through our lives and relationships far more safely, maturely, and effectively.

Once you discover how you can be a confident young woman, my prayer is that you will act on your awareness, address your blind spots, and wear your confidence every day... knowing that confidence is beautiful and so are you!

ACT ON YOUR AWARENESS

Confidence is Beautiful

Day 1: The Confidence of Esther
How do you go from being an orphaned Jewish girl to a confident Persian Queen?

Day 2: My Origin
How does processing my past help reveal blind spots?

Day 3: My Values
How does looking at my present help me understand who I am?

Day 4: My Goals
How does looking into my future help me learn more about what I want to change?

Day 5: My God
Why is it so important to know my God and how do I spend my life getting to know Him better?

Act on Your Awareness--Confidence is Beautiful

The Confidence of Esther

You are invited to come away from the noise of life and invest in your soul. Ask God to quiet your mind and open your ears to hear His message for you today.

Where to begin, where to begin? It's not as easy as you think when, out of sheer anticipation, my heart and mind are both spouting out ideas right and left. That's why I've decided to start with you instead. Please help me get to know you a little better, and perhaps you may gain a few insights as well.

How Badly Do You Want to Be …?

Rate each statement, with 1 meaning it's least important and 5 meaning it's most important. Then circle the two qualities you desire most.

I want to be a brave young woman.

1   2   3   4   5

I want to be a wise young woman.

1   2   3   4   5

I want to be a secure young woman.
1 2 3 4 5
I want to be a beautiful young woman.
1 2 3 4 5
I want to be a strong young woman.
1 2 3 4 5
I want to be a young woman who knows what she cares about.
1 2 3 4 5
I want to be a loved young woman.
1 2 3 4 5
I want to be a young woman who knows her purpose in life.
1 2 3 4 5
I want to be a humble young woman.
1 2 3 4 5
I want to be a young woman who understands herself.
1 2 3 4 5

Thank you for your honesty and for considering what kind of woman you really want to be.

If I was conducting a survey and asked all of you whether you would rather be confident or insecure the rest of your life, I would be wasting my time. Nobody wants to be insecure. Nobody likes to feel insignificant. Nobody wants to always question themselves. Nobody wants to explain their every action or constantly feel defensive. Nobody enjoys avoiding life or just watching it go by. Nobody desires to sabotage their own success. Nobody can handle being self-absorbed 24/7. And yet the land of insecurity is where so many of us women live, both young and old.

However, most of us have never been given a map or directions on how to get out of the land of insecurity. There aren't any high school courses titled "Becoming Confident 101." Nor is there a reality TV show called *Miss Confident Woman*. So where or how do we start?

Making it Clear

What is confidence?

Write two synonyms for the word *confidence:* _____ & _____

Confidence is defined as "the feeling or consciousness of one's powers or of one's reliance on circumstances; the quality or state of being certain." [1]

Over time, I've gained my own definition for confidence. My definition for confidence has four components:

- I am aware of who I am
- I am aware of who God is
- I am aware of who I am in God
- I am aware of what I need to change in order to become all God intended me to be.

What isn't confidence?

Write two antonyms for *confidence*: _____ & _____

Don't be mistaken! When we talk about being confident, we are not talking about arrogance, superiority, having an overbearing personality, being a know-it-all, or being pushy.

Benefits Galore

So, let's take a moment and look at what accompanies confidence. In other words, if you were applying to become a confident woman, what would be the benefits? Here are a few:

role model to others	leader in kindness
possess inner strength	breed goodwill
create atmosphere of harmony	mature lover of people
involved in healthy relationships	courage to dream
respect for personal boundaries	free from chains of insecurity
increased performance	emotional maturity
courage to fail	improves health
courage to succeed	

Doesn't that sound like the most amazing benefits package out there? All I can say is that we should be trying to cut to the front of the line to get these benefits!

Gaze into the truths of God's Word and take note of what resonates with you.

A Special Introduction

Let me introduce you to a woman who I believe possesses all four components of confidence--though not perfectly mind you--an orphaned Jewish girl who came out of nowhere and grew into a confident Persian queen. Her birth name was Hadassah, but she became Queen Esther, a woman who wore her beauty.

We don't have much time, as we technically could spend months studying this amazing woman. Instead, we will spend this day gleaning as much as we can from her life.

Imagine sitting across from her at a table at Starbucks; you have one hour to talk to her. It will be a time for you to ask questions and for her to share details about the most critical period of her life. She will disclose how she would never have imagined some of the events that occurred during this time and how each of her choices revealed the woman she was destined to be.

She begins by saying, "Let me tell you a little bit about my life **before the palace.**"

List in the margin every truth you find about Esther in Esther 2:5-7. What do you imagine would be some of your heartaches growing up as an orphan in your cousin's home?

She continues by explaining one of the scariest days of her life, the day she was taken to become part of King Ahasuerus' harem **in the palace.**

Read Esther 2:8-20.

Taken against her will from her cousin's home, Esther is taken to the palace to compete in a Persian beauty contest for the position of queen. She is thrust into these new living arrangements under the guardianship of Hegai, the custodian of the women. Esther and the other virgins underwent a twelve-month ritual of purification in preparation to meet the king, who was regarded as being semi divine. This preparatory time was probably not unlike modern-day pageants with classes in protocol, court ritual, makeup and dressing techniques, and skin and hair conditioning. These included "*six months of oil of myrrh and six with perfumes and cosmetics*" (2:12).

Esther, raised without a mother, was now surrounded 24/7 by women all competing for the attention of a man, women who compared themselves with each other every moment of the day, women who perhaps were forging false friendships to get the inside scoop on the competition, and women who would spend every moment of every day focused on their outward beauty.

How might Esther have been feeling about herself at this time? What kind of thoughts may have been going through her mind?

What could keep her from becoming self-absorbed and desiring beauty above all else? How?

As the clock ticked down and her day before the King approached, where did she turn for advice and input? Why do you think this was wise? (2:15)

What did the King think of Esther and what was the result? (2:16-17)

Esther leans across the table and whispers to you, "Once I was queen, you wouldn't believe the things I began to hear behind closed doors. Yes, I became **aware of the palace dealings**."

Why hadn't Esther revealed her nationality yet? (2:20)

What was the first secret Esther learned as queen? (2:21-23)

As time marched on, King Ahasuerus promoted Haman to prime minister. Haman planned to kill not just Mordecai, who as a prestigious Jew sat at the gate, but all the Jews in the empire. He obtained King Ahasuerus' permission to execute this plan, against payment of ten thousand silver talents, and he cast lots to choose the date on which to do this--the thirteenth of the month of Adar. On that day, everyone in the empire was free to slaughter the Jews and steal their property. When Mordecai found out about the plot, he and all the Jews went into mourning. Mordecai informed Esther what had happened and told her to intercede with the King.

Read Esther 4:1-17. What was Esther asked to do in verses 11-14? What was the risk that accompanied it?

In verse 14, what did Mordecai propose to Esther about her placement in the palace?

Esther takes a deep breath, sitting a little taller on her stool, and begins to share with you how she **chose to exert her palace influence** in order to save her people.

After facing the reality of death for herself or death for her nation (which would still include her if found out), what did Esther decide to do? (4:16)

After three days of fasting, she bravely put on her royal robes and did what was virtually unheard of in that culture; she boldly approached the king. He miraculously extended his golden scepter to Esther. This simple act signaled that she was being royally accepted and would not be punished by death.

With the king's attention and grace, she invited him and Haman to a feast that she had prepared for them. They attended and the king inquired about her petition, offering up to half of his kingdom. Esther remained silent about her request and, instead, asked them to attend another banquet at which she would tell the king the reason for her request. (5:8)

Meanwhile, Haman was offended again by Mordecai's resistance to bow down to him at the gates, and Haman consulted with his family and friends. With his sense of entitlement and his wife's suggestion, he built gallows for Mordecai.

That night, the king suffered from insomnia and ordered the court records be opened and read to him. Within the reading, he heard of the life-saving service for which Mordecai had never been recognized and wanted to correct the situation. At that moment, Haman appeared to ask whether the king might hang Mordecai, but before he could make his request, the King asked Haman what should be done for a man that the king wished to publicly honor. Thinking the king was referring to him, Haman said the man should be dressed in a royal robe, ride on one of his horses, and have one of the king's nobles lead him around in the city square so all could proclaim him. To his horror, the King told Haman to do that for Mordecai. Haman obeyed but was humiliated.

Read Esther 7:1-6. What does Esther finally reveal about herself? What does she reveal about Haman? And what does she ask of the King?

Overcome by rage, the King left the room while Haman stayed behind and begged Esther for his life, falling upon her in desperation. The king came back at this moment and thought Haman was somehow attacking the queen, which made him even angrier than before. He ordered Haman hung on the gallows that Haman had prepared for Mordecai. What a turn of events!

The previous decree against the Jews could not be revoked, but the king created a new decree that the Jews could defend themselves during the attacks. As a result, on 13 Adar (the twelfth month in the Jewish calendar), five hundred attackers and Haman's ten sons were killed, followed by a Jewish slaughter of seventy-five thousand Persians, although they took no plunder. Esther sent out a letter instituting an annual commemoration of the Jewish people's redemption, a holiday called Purim.

Esther checks the time and apologizes because she needs to take off, but it's been an amazing visit. She thanks you for listening to her story.

Esther's Confident Beauty

Within each category, underline the characteristics of Esther that impressed you the most.

She could say, "I am aware of who I am."

- She was authentic - knew where she came from and didn't feel like she had something to prove. (2:7-10)
- She was humble - in spite of being thrust into a harem where women got what they wanted. (2:44-45)
- She had gracious elegance. (2:9)

- She took responsibility for herself - she spoke to the King and she revealed Haman. (7:6)
- She courageously fights for those she cares about. (4:1-17)

She could say, "I am aware of who God is."

- He led her - when to speak up, when to be quiet, when to listen, how much to say, what to say. (5:1-8, 7:1-4)
- He asked for obedience - it wasn't her job to figure out how God was going to reconcile this. (Chapters 2-8)
- He used her past, her relationships, and her position - all for His sovereign destiny. (Chap. 2-8)
- He empowered her through fasting and prayer. (4:3, 4:16)
- He asked for her faith to go deeper - looking for her to totally trust Him. (Chapters 4-8)

She could say, "I am aware of who I am in God."

- She was teachable - she asked for Hegai's advice and she followed Mordecai's requests. (2:10, 2:15, 2:20)
- She knew she was part of a "people". (4:1-17)
- She knew how to deal with her enemy - let God deal with him! (Chapters 6 & 7)
- She used her patience and self-restraint - she waited through all courses of the meal without blurting out that Haman was trying to kill her people and then waited for the second banquet to even bring up the subject. (Chapters 5 and 7)
- She became selfless - "... and if I perish, I perish." (4:16)

She could say, "I am aware of what I need to change in order to be all God intended me to be."

- She learned that humility before God can be very powerful.
- She learned that she needed to listen to others and gain counsel for wisdom. (2:10, 2:15, 2:20)
- She learned that God chooses His servants "for such a time as this" and she needed to make her impact on God's timeline. (4:14-16)
- She learned that she could gain confidence as she obeys. Each time as God shows Himself trustworthy, she can be more courageous in her next act of obedience. (Chapters 4-7)

- She learned to seek her strength from God and not herself. (4:3, 4:16)
- She learned that courage isn't without fear; it's in spite of. (4:7-16)

"Crisis reveals character." – Oswald Chambers

Esther's awareness of herself, her God, and who she was in her God gave her incredible confidence. The same confidence is waiting for you; you just need to learn who you are, who your God is, who you are in your God, and what you need to change to be all that God intended for you to be. Following Esther's example, you can **act on your awareness, wear your confidence, and know that you are beautiful!**

After reflecting on Esther's life and character, write out a prayer to God asking Him for the kind of confident beauty you want to see in your life.

Last Look in the Mirror

Ask yourself the following:

What stands out to you about God and His character today?

What is the one thing that you learned about yourself today?

How do these answers relate to your present life? What could they be saying to your mind, emotions, or will?

Now that God has examined me, what is the one thing I can change/ add/stop or continue growing in?

You did amazing! Please don't be scared by how much we had to cover today. It will be shorter tomorrow. In the meantime, you go girl!

---

[1] "Confidence." Webster's New World College Dictionary Fourth Edition. Fourth Edition 2008. Print.

Act on Your Awareness--Confidence is Beautiful

My Origin

Processing The Past: Know Who You Are

 Place your outside life on "pause" right now. Quiet your spirit. Ask God to help you process your past. Ask Him to help you see it clearly.

Have you ever wondered why you react the way you do to a certain person? Or have you ever considered why you tend to overreact in particular situations? Have you ever thought about why your first impulse is to lie or get angry or withdraw? Ever given any time to think through why you are attracted to young men who treat you horribly? Ever contemplated why you have such a hard time trusting people?

Having an understanding of one's self is vitally important in life. Before you can build healthy relationships, communicate successfully, or lead respectfully, you need to get a handle on who "you" really are. You need to be able to recognize how you will react to disappointment, what triggers your stress and why, and what your defense mechanisms are and where they originated... just to name a few.

Looking in Your Mirror

So, let's go back to your beginnings and start exploring a little...

Share 1-2 childhood dreams about what you wanted to be when you grew up.

What are 3 words that would describe you as a child?

Name 2-3 painful childhood events that impacted you negatively.

Name 2-3 of your happiest memories.

What are 2-3 things that you learned from your parents about how to love others?

Understanding the past, your history, is to appreciate how your story began and gain insight as to why your story is unfolding the way it is. You did not choose where you were born or the family you were born into or how others treated you in the past. You had no control over circumstances or responsibility for other people's choices, but you have complete control over your ability to reflect on your history in order to gain insight and understand yourself better, therefore allowing you to change your present and future.

Looking in the Mirror

Let's take some time to explore the truths we can glean from two different men with two different backgrounds...

The apostle Paul had a rough background.

What can you learn about Paul's upbringing from Acts 22:3-5 and Philippians 3:5?

How did Paul handle himself or what seemed to be his attitude in Acts 7:54-8:1 and Acts 9:1-4?

Yes, Paul's background was full of religion and notoriety, but neither of those equated to richness, depth, or blessing! Originally named Saul, Paul was so entrenched in his rules and zealous traditions that he couldn't see the Truth, even if it smacked him right in the face.

WARNING: Young woman, don't get sucked into the same kind of life Paul had before he met Christ. Religion can lead you to a life of intense emotions and ritualistic expression, but it can never satisfy your soul. Regulations about how to live will distract you from the true source of Abundant Life and Living Water. God created you for a personal relationship with Him, not mere formality. Remember, only God, not religion, can satisfy the cravings of your soul.

Read how God got Paul's attention in Acts 9:1-20.

According to 1 Timothy 1:12-17, what did he need to overcome because of his past?

Let's look at Timothy who had a rich background.

What can you learn about Timothy's upbringing related to the roots of his faith in Acts 16:1-3 and 2 Timothy 1:5,3:15?

Speaking of Timothy's sincere faith, Paul writes in 2 Timothy that it first was deeply "at home" in his grandmother, Eunice, and his mother, Lois. He uses words that paint a picture of this legacy of Timothy's faith as being genuine, deep, and without hypocrisy. It was the most integral part of his life. This rich heritage and the living example of his family bore much fruit in Timothy's life.

Whether your background is rough or rich or somewhere in between, you need to understand how it has impacted you and how God wants to use it for His glory. Both these men understood and appreciated who they were and where they came from, and it made them more effective Christ-followers.

Paul used his negative upbringing in a positive way.

The apostle Paul became one of the greatest missionaries ever to live. He turned all his "negatives" around. He traveled on three missionary journeys throughout Cyprus, Asia Minor, Europe, and Greece, making over 60 stops along the way (Acts 13-20). Understanding what it meant to need a Savior, his heart was bold and "on fire" for the gospel as he lived in light of eternity. Using his Jewish upbringing and teachings, Paul knew how to witness to those still clinging to their cultural religion. And regardless of the success of his ministry, he remained humble; never losing sight of the fact that he was the "*chief of sinners*" (1 Timothy 1:12-17).

Timothy used his rich heritage to make himself stronger.

Timothy, a convert of Paul's ministry, was challenged to "fan into flame" his spiritual gifting from God, as opposed to becoming complacent in his spiritual knowledge. Watching such authentic faith lived out before him, he, too, was known for his incredible loyalty, knowledge of scripture, and faithful service. Even though his father was Greek and he was not required as a Gentile, he was willing to be circumcised in order to minister to the Jews (Acts 16:3). No matter how many times he traveled alongside Paul or how long he led the church at Ephesus, his teachable heart remained desirous of a mentor to guide him in ministry (1Timothy). He never stopped wanting to grow.

Looking in My Mirror

True, there are many things I have wanted to just forget about my past, but I chose not to buy into the lie that "it's easier to just forget your past." Instead, I wanted to learn more about myself by processing my past and the family that raised me. My questions became, "How could I learn from my past?" and "How could I use that knowledge to make me mentally healthier and more emotionally mature?"

Since there aren't enough pages to share all that I've learned as I've gone through this process, I'll just share two to give you some short chapters out of my story.

#1 - After my parents divorced in the early 1970's, my mother had to go back to work full-time, and it wasn't long before I needed to become quite independent. By the time I was in fourth grade, I was making breakfast, getting my brother and I off to school in the morning, and taking care of the both of us after school until our mom got home from work. This independence grew over time until I believed that it was my responsibility to carry everybody else's responsibilities upon my shoulders. In other words, I thought it was my job to fix or solve all the problems within our family.

This led to a young lady who didn't know how to get out from under the immense weight of enabling others.

#2 - Not assured of the love of my parents and thinking that the divorce might somehow be my fault, I decided within my own little world that I would get the highest grades, be the best behaved daughter, and become the star ballerina-- all in order to earn everybody's love and attention. My choices were screaming, "Please love me! Please notice me!" But no matter how hard I tried or how well I performed, it failed to earn me the unconditional love I desperately desired.

This led to a young lady who was caught in perfectionism in order to please others and who bought into the lie that I needed to perform to gain love.

Don't buy into the **lie** that *"my past is my past and has nothing to do with who I am today."*

In fact, Peter Scazzero, author of *Emotionally Healthy Spirituality,* says that "Denying the past's impact on the present is one of the top ten symptoms of unhealthy spirituality." [1]

Looking in Your Mirror Again

Live the **truth** that "I am influenced by my origins, but my past does not define me."

Name two traits/characteristics you like about yourself. Name a significant person/family member who modeled that for you.

Name two traits/characteristics you don't like about yourself. Can you trace either back to a negative experience or a family member who modeled that trait?

How do you and your family respond to conflict? Comfortable or uncomfortable with it? Head on or avoid it? Done privately or publicly? With harsh words and yelling or with the silent treatment? Describe each person's response.

Parents:

Siblings:

You:

Growing up, who did you feel loved by the most? _____

Who do you think felt the most loved by you? _____

Growing up, who did you want to be loved by but didn't feel it? _____

Was there anyone who might have wanted to be loved by you but might not have felt it? _____

Choose one thing from your past that you realize has influenced who you are...

What would be your first step of action to turn that into an asset for your future?

Have you uncovered any possible blind spots? If so, what do you believe God wants to do with this information?

How I've Used What I've Learned

I don't have to be responsible for others for the rest of my life.

I have come to realize at this point in my life that I am *only* responsible for myself (you'll hear this a million times from me). It is ludicrous to think that I actually have power over another person or that I can make their choices for them. Others make their choices and are responsible for each choice they make, and I make my choices in life and I am responsible for each one.

When my son throws a fit because we don't have what he needs for his science project, I remind him that "It's not my responsibility;" when my friend uses guilt to motivate me to do what she wants, I can now say, "No thanks. That's not my responsibility."

Knowing the truth, I now take the weight of other's bad choices and allow it to be their responsibility. I use it as a reminder to carry them, through prayer, to His throne and lay them at His feet for His will to be accomplished in their lives.

I don't have to perform for love any longer.

In college, I realized that I had transferred this "need to perform" from my dad to my Heavenly Father, so that I was trying to earn God's love through obedience versus being obedient out of an overflowing heart of thankfulness. It was exhausting.

Now, I have grown to accept God's unconditional love for me and believe that I could never do anything to make Him love me more. His love for me is whole and complete. This revelation brings such freedom.

So I try to spend far more time resting in His perfect love for me than I do trying to get God to "notice me!" I will never understand His love for me, but I know it's true.

Last Look in the Mirror

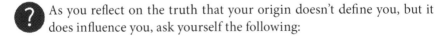 As you reflect on the truth that your origin doesn't define you, but it does influence you, ask yourself the following:

What stands out to you about God and His character today?

What is the one thing that you learned about yourself today?

How do these answers relate to your present life? What could they be saying to your mind, emotions, or will?

What is the one thing I can change/add/stop or continue growing in?

(1)   Peter Scazzero, *Emotionally Healthy Spirituality* (Nashville: Thomas Nelson, 2006, 24.

Act on Your Awareness--Confidence is Beautiful

My Values

Determining Core Values For Your Life: Know Who You Are

We can easily live life at such a pace that we truly never take the time to know ourselves better. Today is the day. Give yourself a gift. Take a moment to ask the Holy Spirit to lead you in this journey.

Meet Bethany Hamilton. Perhaps you know her as the girl who was attacked by a shark, or perhaps you know her as the Soul Surfer. I want to introduce her to you as a young woman who lives out the core values of her life. Yes, the key things she holds dear are what actually drive her from within.

She has been asked, "What does your faith in Jesus Christ mean to you?" And she always replies, without hesitation, one word, "Everything!"

She has also been asked, "What are your key principles for living that you would want to pass on to those looking to you as a role model?" And she has stated, "Do your best in life. Find the good in bad situations. Be kind to others. And, try not to be too cool!" [1]

Those are some great core values and it is evident that she has adopted them as her own because you see them lived out in her life.

Bethany has given her "best" to the surfing world from the time she began competing at age eight, and since then has placed in countless competitions. She took her first National Title in 2005, but she truly achieved her dream when she turned pro in 2007 at the age of seventeen. What an incredible amount of dedication and hard work!

No one can argue the incredibly courageous way Bethany has found the "good in a bad situation," be it in how she was back in the water 26 days after she was attacked by the shark or be it in how she has fully accepted her new body. Her perspective is also proclaimed when she writes. "It helps to know that even when you don't have a clue why something has happened in your life, someone up there has a master plan and is watching over you. It's a tremendous relief to be able to put your trust in God and take the burden off your shoulders." [2]

Her "kindness" has led Bethany to launch her own foundation, Friends of Bethany, which supports shark attack survivors, traumatic amputees, and serves to inspire others through her life story.

Bethany doesn't focus on "being cool," but instead tries very hard to keep her eyes on the Lord and not herself. She gives all the credit of her successes and her ability to overcome tragedy to her relationship with Jesus Christ.

So, now I have a few questions for you to think about...

- "What does your faith in Jesus Christ mean to you?"
- "What are your key principles for living that you would want to pass on to those looking to you as a role model?"
- "Are you living them out?"

21

Looking in a Mirror

People who face their life with a confident purpose are people who know their core values.

Core values are your own personal philosophy or code to live by. They clarify your understanding of who you are, guide you in making decisions or choices, and direct all your relationships.

People don't wear them like the latest fashion or post them in their Facebook status. Your core values aren't displayed, but instead determined deep within you. Like a rudder on a giant ocean vessel, although usually unseen, core values completely navigate your life.

People who understand the true meaning of success have analyzed their personal core values and are living their lives according to what they believe.

Who do you know that lives out their core values? _____

Looking in God's Mirror

Before we take the time to help you determine your core values, let's spend some time discovering what God's core values are for you. This, in turn, could greatly impact your own.

Interestingly enough, in Jesus Christ's final earthly week of ministry, He had four encounters with the religious before His betrayal by them and Judas. During one of those self-serving attempts by the religious leaders to publicly "trap" Jesus, the Lord uses the insincere encounter to reveal what God's true core values are for us today.

Read Matthew 22:34-40. What are God's two core values for you to live by?

Our hearts should be literally molded by these two commandments, and our lives should be driven by these two core values. Sounds simple doesn't it? Just two...really, that's all? Until we take a closer look, two may seem simplistic. Yet, after 30 years of following Christ, I am still working on living out each one increasingly better than I've done in the past.

How I pray for myself, for my husband Mark, and for each one of my children to make each of these our very heartbeat and breath--loving God with every ounce we have and loving others in ways that make Jesus proud.

First Core Value: Loving God

Why does God have the right to claim sole priority in our lives? (Romans 5:8, Galatians 2:20, 1 Corinthians 6:20)

What does God say about Himself? (Exodus 20:4-6, Deuteronomy 4:24)

How do you make your possessive God jealous? How do you make Him feel like He holds second place or third place or even last place?

Think of the last time He felt first in your life. Describe how you felt when loving Him came first.

One of my best friends raised his family with this saying--*"Put God first, life goes best."* He challenged his kids to put God first with their money, and life would go best. Put God first with their time, and life would go best. Put God first in their jobs, and life would go best. Put God first in their friendships, and life would go best. His list has no end to it because the challenge is to put God first in every aspect of your life and you will see that it is the only way for your life to go best.

Second Core Value: Loving Others

This value doesn't stand on its own within this passage. Your love for others is a direct result of your love for God. At seventeen, no one had to convince me that I was an "outsider" looking in, completely unworthy of the love of our Holy God. And, honestly, the longer I serve Him, the more in awe I am of the truth that He accepts me and welcomes me with open arms. There is not a doubt in my mind how unworthy I still am, but He still loves me!

So I desperately want others to feel His unwarranted waterfall of love for them. I want others to know what it feels like to walk into His open arms or crawl into His lap. I have the power of Christ living in me to show them the love of God.

Do you feel more obligated to love others or more excited to love others? Why?

Who are the hardest people for you to love?

What does God say is a great way to love the ones who are hardest to love? (Matthew 5:44, Luke 6:28)

What do you think is the hardest part about your personality to love?

Why can't we separate loving God and loving the people He created? (I John 4:19-20)

Loving other people is never an option for us. It is the greatest hallmark and expression of our love for God Himself. It's gratitude of His death on the cross lived out.

God's two most basic core values are crystal clear, and they affect every choice we will ever make.

Looking in Your Mirror

Now what are your personal core values?

Since most of us have never taken the time or quite know how to analyze what ours actually are, let's do that right now. As you read through this list, think about what's most important to you, what you are most passionate about, what shapes your behavior and what motivates your decisions.

NOTE: Once I discovered my core values, I took my top 15 that I had circled and created my own list of just those. Then I emailed my list of 15 to a few close friends and asked them to choose the top 5 they saw lived out in my life.

It was interesting to see if my life was consistent with what I believed to be the most important. (I now have them framed by my desk as a constant reminder.)

Personal Core Values List

Place a check by any of these values that are important to you. Now read through the ones you have checked and narrow those down to the 15 most important to you. Circle those 15. Okay - read those top 15 values and cross out the 5 that are least critical to you. Again - read through your top 10 and cross out 3 more values that don't motivate you as strongly. Lastly - read through the 7 remaining and cross out 2 more values that you aren't as passionate about. You now have your 5 core values of life! Number them in importance to you. Great job!

Accountability	Fairness	Meaning
Accuracy	Faith	Openness
Adventure	Faithfulness	Patriotism
Beauty	Family	Peace, Non-violence
Calm, quietude, peace	Freedom, Liberty	Personal Growth
Challenge	Friendship	Perseverance
Change	Fun	Pleasure
Charity	Generosity	Power
Commitment	Gentleness	Practicality
Communication	Global view	Preservation
Community	Goodness	Privacy
Competence	Gratitude	Progress
Competition	Hard work	Prosperity, Wealth
Concern for others	Happiness	Punctuality
Continuous	Health	Reliability
improvement	Honor	Resourcefulness
Cooperation	Improvement	Respect for others
Creativity	Independence	Responsiveness
Decisiveness	Individuality	Results-oriented
Determination	Innovation	Safety
Discipline	Integrity	Security
Discovery	Justice	Self-givingness
Diversity	Kindness	Self-thinking
Efficiency	Knowledge	Sensitivity
Enjoyment	Leadership	Simplicity
Equality	Love, Romance	Solving Problems
Excellence	Loyalty	Spirit, Spirituality in life

Stability	Tolerance	Unity
Status	Tradition	Variety
Strength	Tranquility	Wisdom
Systemization	Trust	
Teamwork	Truth	

"If the ladder is not leaning against the right wall, every step we take just gets us to the wrong place faster." - Stephen R. Covey, author of the best- selling book, *The Seven Habits of Highly Effective People*

Sister, make sure your ladder is against the right wall--the wall of your core values.

The difference between being effective and merely surviving is the ability to define and recognize your core values and then integrate them into every aspect of your life. Core values are the foundation that creates more of what you do want and less of what you don't want in your life. They must be present in your daily actions if you want to be truly at peace with yourself and achieve the success you desire.

Last Look in the Mirror

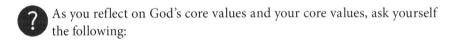 As you reflect on God's core values and your core values, ask yourself the following:

What stands out to you about God and His character today?

What is the one thing that you learned about yourself today?

How do these answers relate to your present life? What could they be saying to your mind, emotions, or will?

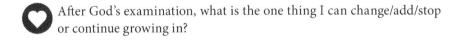 After God's examination, what is the one thing I can change/add/stop or continue growing in?

---

(1) Bethany Hamilton: Soul Surfer, Professional Surfer, Role Model, Inspiration. 2010. Collaboration Reverberation. 2011. <www.bethanyhamilton.com>
(2) Ibid.

Act on Your Awareness--Confidence is Beautiful

My Goals

Intentional About The Future: Know Who You Are

 Jesus has been waiting for this time together. Prepare your heart to meet with Him. He is anticipating what you two will dialogue about.

"I am not a has-been. I am a will be." - Lauren Bacall

You are not a has-been. You are a "will be." But the question before you, at this point on your journey to truly understand yourself, is "Who will you be?"

The Bad News: If you have never taken the time to imagine how you want to be treated within relationships, or set goals for what you want to do with your dreams, or chosen the main character qualities you desire to be known for, then I am sorry to tell you that the odds are you will never achieve those things. You will join the masses who allow life to shape them. And you will look back with regret wondering why life has felt less than it should.

The Good News: You can start at this very moment to change the future. According to an African proverb, "Tomorrow belongs to the people who prepare for it today." So are you ready? Excited? Are you willing to prepare for who you want to be in the next chapter of your life? Who you want to be in the next five years? In ten years? Let's get started.

Looking in God's Mirror

No one is more concerned about your future than God is, and He has a lot to say about it. Settle in--the first place we're going to start is with what God has to say about goal setting.

What do Proverbs 21:5 and Luke 14:28-31 have to say about the principle of planning ahead?

Wisdom tells us to diligently sow strategies for our future. Paul challenged us to keep our focus on our goal and not get sidetracked or dragged down by our past. Luke admonished us that there is an order to accomplishing things that always begins with first determining the answers to questions ahead of time.

When it comes to fixing our eyes on the future, there's a man who instantly comes to my mind, the apostle Paul, my New Testament hero! Talk about a man who declared how he wanted to live and then lived it. I have such deep admiration of his boldness with the gospel and his laser-focused living. (I'd love either of those things to be said about me someday.) He was a man who lived every moment in light of eternity.

Read Philippians 3:7-14.

From verses 10-11, there are 3 goals he set his sights on: (1) Experiencing the power of Christ's resurrection, (2) Becoming a partner with Jesus in His suffering, and (3) Being conformed to His death. Let's see what Paul did to reach his goals.

1st Goal: How did Paul **experience Christ's power** in these verses?

1 Corinthians 2:4-5

2 Corinthians 12:8-10

2nd Goal: How did Paul **partner in Jesus's suffering** in these verses?

2 Corinthians 11:23-33

Romans 8:17

3rd Goal: How did Paul **conform to Christ's death** in these verses?

Philippians 1:21-22

Galatians 2:20

No one can deny that Paul determined the kind of man he wanted to be for God and then his life became the living proof.

Looking in Your Mirror

Remember, you are not a "has been" either--you are a "will be."

Don't ever buy into the **lie** that you cannot change or it's too late!

With God ALL things are possible. Not some things, not several things, not many things, not a few things...ALL things (Job 42:1-2). You are a new creation with the potential for anything imaginable (2 Corinthians 5:17), and every day God's mercy is new just for you (Lamentations 3:22-23).

Hold on tightly to the **truth,** it's never too late to start making the right choices!

So, hello Miss "Will Be," here's your chance--start thinking about what kind of a woman you want to be for God.

Choose 3 goals for what kind of friend you want to be.

As a future wife, what are the 5 most critical traits you want to offer your husband?

Determine 1 physical goal for yourself.

Determine 1 spiritual goal for yourself.

Create 2 goals for yourself as a citizen/servant that will impact your community or this world.

You get 3 words written on your tombstone, what would you like them to be?

Someone once said, "If you aim at nothing, you'll hit it every time." We have to determine, think about, and pursue the kind of woman God has called each of us to be. We have to be intentional with our futures.

My prayer is that each of us, like Paul, would learn to live in light of eternity.

Last Look in the Mirror

 Reflect and ask yourself the following:

What stands out to you about God and His character today?

What is the one thing that you learned about yourself today?

How do these answers relate to your present life? What could they be saying to your mind, emotions, or will?

After God's examination, what is the one thing I can change/add/stop or continue growing in?

Way to go lady! You have looked at your past, your present, and your future. You've only got one more day for the week. I hope you're learning lots about yourself because you are doing great!

Act on Your Awareness--Confidence is Beautiful

My God

Knowing Him & The Pursuit Thereof: Know Who God Is

God has been counting down the moments to this one. He loves to reveal Himself to those who long to see Him...more than you know. Close your eyes and ask to see Him and a glimpse of His glory.

I grew up ignorant about God. Our family never went to church. We never prayed. We never talked about anything spiritual. Although I do remember my grandma Crisp giving all of us grandkids a white KJV Bible one Christmas. I started reading in Genesis, but I couldn't understand it. So, I gave up.

By the age of 10, I began having horrible nightmares involving death. It was the exact same nightmare over and over. I dreamt that I could see the earth from a side view and at the very top was my grave full of bones. All night long, people of all ages would pop up out of the grave, run around the earth, and fall back into the grave as a pile of bones. I can remember asking my mom, "What happens after you die?" To this day, I can't remember how she answered me.

I remember asking my babysitter the same question and then our neighbors. Whatever I was told, it didn't satisfy my questioning.

A few years later, I began going to church each Sunday with whichever neighbor would take me. I was searching for answers to an inner emptiness. I found myself believing in a God, but a religious God that just existed somewhere out there in heaven. I thought that if I went to show Him respect each Sunday and tried to be a good girl that would satisfy Him.

I was blind to the truth that I still didn't know God. I had no idea what would satisfy Him. I was clueless that He wanted a relationship with me--that He didn't want to just see me every Sunday, but walk with me every moment of my life.

He already knew everything about me since He was the One who "knitted me together in my mother's womb." He knew every nook and cranny of my heart, I just didn't know Him!

In any relationship, it's far easier to grow apart than it is to grow closer. As a television co-host, I spent seven years interviewing relationship experts, researching and reading countless books on relationships, and worked alongside a man who was Canada's Relationship Coach. It became critically clear how purposeful we must be within our relationships. It's far easier to enjoy honeymoon phases, when you can't wait to put effort towards each other, than it is to endure the dry and distant times.

Don't buy into the **lie** that relationships just come naturally or without effort.

As a woman in her late 40s, I am extremely intentional about the relationships that matter in my life. I can honestly say that I pursue, I evaluate, I set goals for, I make changes to, and I am deeply blessed by each rich, real relationship. These relationships are not perfect and do not always go smoothly. (Remember I have real relationships.) But, I keep re-engaging in each of these important relationships...trying to get to know the one I love better and constantly understanding myself more.

The relationship that matters most to me is my relationship with my Lord and Savior, Jesus Christ. Even more than my relationship with my amazing husband, Mark, my love for God comes first. Once you know this about me, it explains one of my life's chief goals--to know God. He is the One I want to know the most, and so I will pursue Him until the day He takes me home. I will make every effort to understand Him and all the amazing facets of His character.

Looking in God's Mirror

All of mankind was created for relationships--relationships with each other and a relationship with God. He has so much to say about wanting to be close to you.

How can you see His desire for a relationship with you in Psalms 139:1-18?

God could have created us predestined to love Him and to want to be close to Him, but He didn't. I love that God didn't choose to make us robots or puppets. He gave each of us a free will to make our own choices.

How do you see that in Deuteronomy 30:15-20?

The Holy One could have wanted to be the ultimate leader of a religion with each one of us His loyal subjects. We would just be required to go through motions and rituals in order to satisfy Him. It would be void of emotion and closeness and desires--it would be void of heart.

How does Micah show us otherwise in Micah 6:6-8?

Again, the only "rite" that God delivers into our hands in this lifetime is in the following verse.

> *"Yet to all who did receive him, to those who believed in his name,*
> *he gave the right to become children of God."* John 1:12

From the first word in Genesis to the last word in Revelation, God paints the picture with a scarlet paint brush of His desire to have a relationship with each one of us. He makes it abundantly clear that He knows our hearts inside and out, but do you know His heart? Do you think that it's important to Him that you know Him?

What does Jeremiah 9:23-24 say?

Looking in Your Mirror

How well do you think you know your God?

Let's pretend that you are responsible for filling out God's profile for His new Facebook page. Let's see how you do....

NAME:

HOMETOWN:

BIRTHDAY:

RELIGIOUS VIEWS:

POLITICAL VIEWS:

LIKES:

DISLIKES:

INTERESTS:

Looking in God's Mirror

If you are anything like me, then you realize that you have a long way to go when it comes to knowing our infinite God. There won't be enough days on this earth to fully know Him, if that is even humanly possible. So, in the meantime, we *"press on...press on to know Him"* more and more each day (Hosea 6:3).

And if you are anything like me, you've got a question on the tip of your tongue right now--"How? How do we do that?"

We build a relationship with God in the same way we build a relationship with anybody else.

We spend time talking and listening to each other, asking questions until we understand one another. We hang out together, plan to do things together, and watch each other in all different sorts of life situations. Coincidentally, the

Bible teaches the same things about how we can grow in our understanding of and connection with our Father.

Talking to God

Prayer is simply talking to God. It is speaking from your heart, freely, spontaneously, and using your own words. The Bible has a lot to say about prayer, but what can you learn from the following verses?

Matthew 6:5-13

Romans 8:26-27

Listening to God

Our Western American culture can be one of the noisiest places on earth, which can make the skill of listening seem almost impossible at times. Although it may be difficult for us, does God expect us to find the quiet somehow and listen to Him?

1 Kings 19:11-13

John 10:3-4, 27

The only way I can hear God's voice is when I engage in quietness. Most people expect God to answer them verbally, right out of the heavens, but that isn't the way God operates. God speaks to a person's heart, to their mind, and to their sense of moral righteousness and fairness. It's not a verbal voice we are waiting to hear, but the still, small voice of our Shepherd that speaks to us in His Word, through His Holy Spirit, and many times through mature brothers and sisters in Christ.

Spending Time with God in His Word

There is absolutely no better way to know God than to know His Word. We need to live inside the pages of His love letter, the Bible. These words of Scripture are living and the very breath of God. They are God's heart in book form. Check out Joshua 1:8 and note the priority we need to place on spending time with God in His Word.

See a few glimpses of who God is in His Word and record what you see:

Ecclesiastes 12:14

Isaiah 40:25-26. 28

Isaiah 54:10

We will never know God if we don't make His Word our priority. Life will always be busy. We cannot wait to find the time; we must make the time.

Spending Time with God's Family

When my husband and I were dating in college, we thought it wise that before we considered talking about marriage, we really needed to meet each other's families. We knew that our eyes would be opened to understand a whole lot more about one another if we did. You see, the more you hang out with someone's family, the more you learn about a person. God also wants us to learn more about His heart from our spiritual family, the Church.

As we share this journey of life, Psalms teaches us that we are supposed to continually go into the temple and declare His praises, tell one another how He is working and what He is teaching us. This gives us, as listeners, even more insight into His glorious character.

Hebrews 10:25 exhorts us to what?

Hold on tightly to the **truth** that love takes effort.

Make effort to know your God, sweet sisters of mine. I know that sin gets in the way and makes us feel a million miles away from God. That's what sin does--it separates. And I know that we can slowly drift away with one compromise after another. And I know that there are times when we have no feelings for

God, like we're just going through the motions. I have experienced each and every one of those situations. However, I am here to stand and shout as loud as I can that you don't have to give into those times! In the same way that my husband and I have fought our way back to each other when we've been distant or there is hurt between us; we always need to keep fighting our way back to God. He begs us to *"draw near and He will draw near to you"* (James 4:8). I can honestly say that each time my husband and I have fought for our relationship; we have gone to deeper and richer places. It all becomes part of our shared history. Don't you want that to be said of you and your Father God?

Confess your sin and don't let anything come between you and your Lord. Stop compromising and reconnect with God's people and God's Word. Choose to live by faith and not by emotions; emotions can never be trusted and God can never forsake you. Ask God for the love to love Him. Ask God for a deep desire to want Him above all others. Ask God for the hunger to know Him.

Looking in Your Mirror

Rate how you are doing with talking to God to develop deeper communication.
1   2   3   4   5   6   7   8   9   10

Rate how you are doing at listening to God to hear Him more effectively
1   2   3   4   5   6   7   8   9   10

Rate how you are doing at spending time in His Word to know Him more.
1   2   3   4   5   6   7   8   9   10

Rate how you are doing at making it a priority to spend time with His family.
1   2   3   4   5   6   7   8   9   10

What are 2 specific things you would like to start doing to get to know your God better?

Last Look in the Mirror

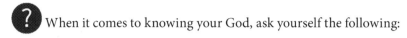 When it comes to knowing your God, ask yourself the following:

What stands out to you about God and His character today?

What is the one thing that you learned about yourself today?

How do these answers relate to your present life? What could they be saying to your mind, emotions, or will?

After God's examination, what is the one thing I can change/add/stop or continue growing in?

WRAP UP TO YOUR
FIRST WEEK OF STUDY

Confidence is awareness of who you are, who God is, who you are in God, and what you need to change in order to become all God wants you to be. You have just taken a purposeful look at who you are according to your past and asked yourself if there are any blind spots. You looked at your present life to gain more self-understanding. You looked into your future through the eyes of "what needs to change" and "who do I want to be?" Then you spent a day understanding how critical it is to spend the rest of your life getting to know your God and His heart. With that foundation in place, it's time to seek out some of the incredible identities that belong to you as God's child. Next week, you will seek to answer the question, "Who am I in Jesus Christ?"

Looking Toward Your Second Week of Study

In the teenage years, you began your quest for identity and most of you considered it a struggle. It was common for you to search for it through prestige--wearing the right clothes, having the right accessories, buying the right technology. You may have engaged in practices associated with adulthood—such as smoking, drinking, drugs, and sexual activity. Or perhaps you rebelled against anything associated with your parents and authority giving you a sense of separation as you searched for your identity.

Young adult women are constantly trying to define and redefine themselves in relation to others, causing them to be very cliquish. They try to strengthen their own identities by excluding those who are not like themselves. These struggles reveal the truth that you are searching in the wrong places for your identity.

You will only find your true identity in Jesus Christ. Knowing who you are in Him will give you what you want most--a sense of value, belonging, and destiny. Have a blast this week soaking in the reality of who you really are!

ACT ON YOUR AWARENESS

Confidence is Beautiful

DAY 6: My Identity
What does it mean to know you are a daughter of the King?

DAY 7: My Humility
What does it mean to know you are a justified sinner?

DAY 8: My Beauty
What does it mean to know that you are His unique masterpiece?

DAY 9: My Wedding
What does it mean to know that you are His bride?

DAY 10: My Security
What does it mean to know that you are a citizen of heaven?

Act on Your Awareness--Confidence is Beautiful

My Identity

Daughter of the King: Know Who You Are In God

 Deep breath. Slow down. Enter His majestic throne room and ask for this time to be meaningful at a soul level.

Don't buy into the **lie** that your life determines your identity.

WARNING: This could be you in the future!

You are 25 years old walking down the aisle to the wrong guy--at least that's the thought going on inside of your head. You don't know how you got here or why it's so important to you to keep up appearances and please everybody around you. Most of your girlfriends have already gotten married and they look like they are happy. This whole thing just doesn't feel like you thought it was supposed to.

You are 33 years old and have more talents than most people can imagine. You love to serve and people are constantly asking you to be in charge of something. Your creativity and administrative skills are coveted. But you've had it! People don't listen to some of your greatest ideas--they just want to do it the way they've always done it in the past. Everybody takes advantage of you, no one thanks you, and you're exhausted. So you cut ties and completely pull back from committees and teams and friends. After a while, you miss it and you re-engage. The problem is you've been repeating this cycle for as long as you can remember and nothing changes.

You are 41 years old and have been married to your college sweetheart for almost 20 years. Your husband has been the most romantic and faithful guy around. How can you be so blessed? Then he gets a new administrative assistant at his company who works side-by-side with him. She is a gorgeous blonde with a body that has never carried a baby. She's recently divorced and you can't believe the things you start imagining. Jealousy consumes you and if someone ever told you that you would be horribly mean to a stranger who has never done anything to you, you would call them a liar. Your husband has never given you a reason to doubt him, but you've already judged, tried, and convicted him in your mind. You hate life right now.

Young lady, please don't let this be you. Please settle your identity BEFORE you go off to college, BEFORE you choose a career, and BEFORE you decide to marry!

Cling to the **truth** that your identity determines your life.

Each of these women has allowed her life to determine her identity. And, frankly, most women do. But you can be different and you can be miles ahead of where I was when I left home. You don't have to be deeply insecure not knowing who you really are, and hoping you'll find yourself along the way. You can hold fast to the truth that you are a daughter of the King of Kings. In other words, if you are a Christ-follower, you are officially a princess.

Which Disney Princess are You?

Let us have a little fun for a moment. Read through and circle the list of descriptive words that comes closest to describing you.

Princess #1

Listens to Love Songs	Is Persistent
Princess means Happily Ever After	Enjoys a Spring Formal

Likes Home Economics	Countryside
Wants a Loving Home	Singing Lessons
Likes Mice	Comfortable

Princess #2

Listens to Classical music	Wants an Enchanted Home
Princess means a Fairytale Wedding	Likes Horses
Is Intelligent	Mountains
Enjoys a Masquerade Ball	Debate Team
Likes World History	Preppy

Princess #3

Listens to Opera	Wants a Cozy home
Princess means Ruling	Likes Squirrels
Over a Kingdom	Forest
Is Innocent	Cooking
Enjoys a Welcome Home Party	Casual
Likes Music	

Princess #4

Listens to Show Tunes	Wants a home Far Away
Princess means Being Rescued	Likes Tigers
Is Kind	Dessert
Enjoys a Parade	Gymnastics
Likes Art	Trendy

Princess #5

Listens to Renaissance Music	Wants a Grand Home
Princess means True Love's Kiss	Likes Doves
Is Gracious	Wooded Glen
Enjoys a Sweet 16 Party	Sewing Lessons
Likes English	British

Princess #6

Listens to Reggae	Wants a home Overlooking Water
Princess means Enchanted Objects	Likes Fish
Is Inquisitive	Tropical Island
Enjoys a Wedding	Swim Team
Likes Biology	Rocker

So, which one are you? #1 – Cinderella, #2 – Belle, #3 - Snow White, #4 – Jasmine, #5 - Sleeping Beauty, #6 - Ariel

How fun and cool would it be to work at Disneyland and get to put on your princess costume each day, have little girls look at you with the biggest eyes you've ever seen, and older girls hug you like they never want to let you go! Just the opportunity of dressing up and pretending to be a Princess for a few hours a day is beyond our imagination. Young women, you don't have to pretend-- you are the real thing. As a Christian, you are part of the royal family of the universe!

Looking in God's Mirror

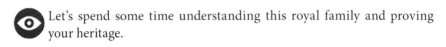 Let's spend some time understanding this royal family and proving your heritage.

What is one of God's many titles according to Revelation 17:14 and 19:16?

Use Ephesians 1:5 and Galatians 3:26 to show who you are once you have received Jesus as your Savior.

Choosing to adopt you indicates that He has chosen to be your father. What do you learn about Him as your Father in Romans 8:15 and 1 John 3:1?

(*Av* is the Hebrew word for "father." *Abba* denotes a more intimate and reverent term of "O father.")

Simply put - God is the _____.
He has adopted me as His _____.
That makes me a _____.

God doesn't want you to doubt or question this. What does He say in 1 John 5:11-13?

As a princess, daughter of the King, you now belong to His royal family. This meets such a deep need of ours as women--to belong and to feel special.

According to Abraham Maslow's Hierarchy of Human Needs, the need to belong--desire for interpersonal attachments--is a fundamental human motivation.[1] God has created the "family" as His primary source to meet this need, but that is not always the case. Why do you think "gangs" have such a powerful draw to young kids with no family ties? It's because their soul is craving to belong to something or someone.

As women, we are not exempt. Regardless of whether your family has answered your soul's craving for belonging, God's family does. These verses declare how strongly He feels about you and this family of His.

What do you learn from Isaiah 41:8-10 and Romans 8:38-39 about how God feels about His family?

In the family of God, according to Romans 12:9-10 and Philippians 2:1-3, how are we to treat each other?

Write a love note to God expressing how this all makes you feel.

Looking in My Mirror

The **Lie**: Your life determines your identity.
The **Truth**: Your identity determines your life.

Have you ever felt like you were on the outside looking in? I grew up feeling that way most of the time. As a child I stood on the "outside" of my best friend's life looking "in" on her family. I wanted to be her. I remember sitting on the couch watching her mother comb and put ribbons in her hair each morning before we would walk to school. I observed how they sat as family at their table for breakfast, lunch, and dinner. I envied how her mother was always home.

Then, as a teen who just had moved to a new high school with a new step-family, I got invited to a youth group. For the next few years, I found myself once again feeling like I was on the outside looking in on this youth group family of teenagers. How do I get into the inner circle? How can I be close to the Youth Pastor? How do I get invited to early morning prayer times? How can I get discipled one-on-one?

It was almost like I was living in some invisible bubble where I could only observe close relationships but not actually be a part of them. I desperately wanted to belong. I had believed the lie for far too long. My identity had nothing to do with being a child of divorce, my friends, my moving, my high school, or my youth group. It had everything to do with Jesus Christ, whom I met at the age of 17, and I have never been the same since.

Looking in Your Mirror

Let's review the **lie** and the **truth** for today--<u>say</u> the **lie** and <u>write</u> the **truth** out below.

Your identity as a daughter of the King of Kings should make you a confident woman. "But, I don't feel confident just because I know that," you might say. I agree. There is a huge difference between knowing something as a fact and choosing to believe in something. A dear friend of mine says, "You do what you do because you believe what you believe." In other words, your core beliefs are the foundation that, in turn, directly impact how you behave.

If you were to observe me for a week--watched my choices, noted my priorities, listened in on my conversations, possibly even heard some of my inner thoughts--you would be able to tell me what I really believed about myself because my behavior reflects my beliefs.

Something to think about: If I observed your life the past two weeks, what would I conclude you believe about yourself?

Let me illustrate this another way: Britain has a new princess, Miss Kate Middleton, as of July 29, 2011. How long do you think it took before she began acting like a princess? Do you think she only remembers that she is a princess when she looks at her ring? Maybe she only remembers when she looks at her wedding photos and talks about the ceremony?

Or, perhaps, she thought long and hard about what it would mean to marry Prince William and marry into the Royal Family of Britain. I imagine she had numerous considerations about what this step would look like for every day of the rest of her life. After all the pros and cons, she chose to marry the love of her life. I honestly don't think there will ever come a morning when she will wake up having forgotten her identity, and then suddenly recall later, "Oh my goodness, I forgot! That's right...I'm a princess." There might be many moments of being overwhelmed with the pressures associated with her title and many others pinching herself to see if it's all real, but never a moment of doubt. Today, she knows exactly who she is. She believes it, and she lives it.

Precious sisters, if you are a daughter of the King of Kings, you can pinch yourself every single day of the rest of your life, but you better be living like you KNOW and BELIEVE who you are! You cannot compare the smallness of being a princess of a single country for a short span, like Kate, with being a princess of the King of the Universe for eternity, like you.

What do you still need to believe in order to wake up confident?

What could you do to start reminding yourself daily of your identity?

How could we, as fellow women and sisters, remind each other of this more?

As my children grew up leaving for school in the morning, I had a phrase that I would always say as each one walked out the door of our home, "Never forget who you belong to!" To this day, I still will remind them as they drive away or head off to college, "Always remember who you belong to--the Mark Rayburn family and God Himself."

Now, I am saying it to you sweet girl, "Always remember who you belong to--every day and every moment of your life."

Last Look in the Mirror

Knowing that you are a princess, ask yourself the following:

What stands out to you about God and His character today?

What is the one thing that you learned about yourself today?

How do these answers relate to your present life? What could they be saying to your mind, emotions, or will?

After looking into His mirror, what is the one thing I can change/add/ stop or continue growing in?

¹ Wikipedia contributors. "Maslow's hierarchy of needs." *Wikipedia, The Free Encyclopedia*. Wikipedia, The Free Encyclopedia, 11 Dec. 2013. Web. 16 Dec. 2013.

Act on Your Awareness--Confidence is Beautiful

My Humility

Justified Sinner: Know Who You Are In God

Selah. It means to pause and consider. We are going to need that today. Our study is going to cover one of those mighty big truths that is difficult to grasp. So, please, *selah*.

She Just Doesn't Like Me

Have you ever had someone not like you and you don't know why? You think to yourself, "Did I miss something here? I just don't get this." Well, I went to Pinole Junior High where I was bullied by a particular group of girls in the 7th grade. I never understood it--and I still don't. I had not done anything to them, and yet they treated me like I was their adversary. They pushed me around, called me names, smeared their lunch food on me, and degraded me at every opportunity. Let me be the first to tell you that it's not fun to have an enemy, especially when there is no apparent reason.

To this day, being a very relational woman, I cannot stand it when there is something between myself and someone I care about. Instantly, my world is not right, and all I seem to be able to focus on is getting it worked out as soon as possible so we can be "okay" again. I won't forsake the truth, I'm willing to have those "hard conversations," and I will make every effort to bring peace back to the relationship because my relationships are one of the most important things in my life.

Quick Look in the Mirror

Is there anyone you are "at odds" with right now? If yes, what have you done to try to make peace?

God calls us to be peacemakers in Matthew 5:9. The Greek word for peace implies that it is more than the absence of strife but that there has been some sort of agreement on terms; a reconciliation which is far more than merely keeping peace.

Are you more of a peacekeeper or peacemaker? _____

What do you need to do in order to live the life of a peacemaker and not be a "door mat?"

At Odds or at Peace?

Did you realize that from the moment you took your first breath out of your mother's womb, you were at odds with Someone. From the first time you sinned, you had an enemy, but not who you might think. I am talking about the enmity between the Holy Creator of this world and you.

From the first moment that I began to wonder about this, I was very unsettled in my soul. There was something separating me from God from the moment I was born: I just couldn't cozy up to Him and waltz right into His arms? In my imagination and my assumptions, He seemed like He would be such a big, loving God. Then I learned what separated us--what made us enemies--was MY SIN! Wow! It wasn't like being bullied in junior high school where there was no reason whatsoever. I was the reason. That blew me away...but it also made sense. No one needed to convince me of my sin, my self-driven life, or my ugliness before a Holy God. I had spent enough days crying into my mirror with mascara-stained cheeks, hating myself and the choices I had made. I hated myself and had lost all hope, to the point of planning my suicide. So, if there was something I could do about making this "right," then I was on a quest to find out.

I learned that His big love (bigger than the imagination could even dream up) is what sent Jesus Christ to face His Father's wrath which had been stored up towards sin and sinners since time began. He would become the very sin that God hated, have His Father forsake Him, die the most torturous death possible, be buried, and rise again three days later, thereby conquering the power of death and offering people a new reconciled position with Him through the indwelling of the Holy Spirit. And this was in spite of every sin they had ever committed and every sin they ever would commit in their lifetime. I discovered that there was just one thing that brings peace between Almighty God and mankind-- Jesus Christ. Yet, although I could believe He did that for everybody else, I had a hard time swallowing that He could do that for me. Really? Seriously me?

One beautiful morning, while out walking on a mountain road in Lake Tahoe, I looked around at His creation and was silenced by His majesty. He became so real to me in that moment that I finally heard Him and believed Him when He said, "Yes, Christie Lee ... for you, my precious girl." He died for me. I began crying and just couldn't stop. Humbled and overwhelmed, I became His daughter.

In Isaiah 27:5 God declares, "Let them make peace with Me."

How did you realize that Jesus became sin and died to offer you peace with God? Or, are you still trying to understand that?

Looking in God's Mirror

 Let's explore the truth about who we really are and what we really deserve.

What does creation do in response to Creator God?

The Water - Job 12:15
The Wind - Mark 4:37-41
The Mountains - Psalms 104:32

What does man do in response to Creator God? Genesis 3:1-13, 22-24 & Romans 3:23

Don't you find it fascinating that creation obeys and follows the Creator God, but man doesn't? Man chooses autonomy, living life according to his terms. Every choice of independence, living as if God doesn't exist, is sin.

What does sin do in our lives? Isaiah 59:2, Ephesians 4:18

What is the punishment for our sin? What are our consequences? Romans 6:23, Matthew 25:46

As sinners, what is our relationship to Almighty God? Ephesians 2:1-3, Galatians 3:10-11

David Platt, author of *Radical*, writes, "There is absolutely nothing we can do to come to God. We can't manufacture salvation. We can't program it. We can't produce it. We can't even initiate it. God has to open our eyes, set us free, overcome our evil, and appease His wrath. He has to come to us." [1]

Now we get to the incredibly good news of the Gospel!

What is the Good News according to Romans 3:26 and 2 Corinthians 5:21?

What must we do to be justified? Romans 10:9-13

As justified sinners, what comes with our new standing in Christ? Romans 5:1 & 8:1,38-39

One of the most incredible statistics I've ever heard is that 90% of mental patients could be released from psychiatric hospitals if their guilt could just somehow be dealt with! Precious sister, the stain of our guilt has been forever removed!

The Court Room & the Trial

Imagine walking through the doors into a courthouse because you received a summons with today's date, your name, and the huge reminder of your verdict of "Guilty" written across it. You slowly step up to the clerk to report in and she hands you the necessary paperwork to take before the Judge. She gives you directions to the courtroom you have been assigned to and you find it far too easily. You were hoping you could somehow draw this out longer--your sentencing. Even with the heaviness on your heart and the sickness in your stomach, you aren't ready for the emotions that begin to swirl inside of you as you open the door and the ominous air greets you.

There is no one else in the courtroom but you, so you take a hard, wooden seat and wait in the silence that about kills you. (Funny choice of words, since you already know what the sentence will be--death.) How could this day already be here? Life has gone so fast up till this point.

The Accuser walks in first. He isn't what you pictured him to be at all. He's very good looking, dressed in an Armani suit and carrying a Louis Vuitton briefcase. He sets his briefcase down, efficiently opens it like he's done it a million times before, pulls out a stack of papers and takes a seat.

The Judge walks in next with His flowing robe, regal ways, and takes His respected chair of complete authority.

Without a moment's hesitation, the Accuser stands and begins with the smoothest, lulling tone you've ever heard. If you weren't paying close attention, you would think he was singing your praises. But, as you listen more closely and his tone begins to increase in volume and turn vile, he seems to relish reading off every offense you have ever committed or even thought about committing. Hearing your sins read out loud is the most humiliating thing you have ever experienced. It feels like you've brought the ugliest, filthiest things into the presence of the most pristine, respected, and righteous One. You just want to get this over with and hear your punishment of death.

Then, from the left, walks in the Innocent One. You hadn't even known He was in the room up to this point. He boldly walks straight up to the Judge Himself, fully ignoring the Accuser's rant, and whispers something in the Judge's ear. The Judge loudly raps his gavel on the wood and the Accuser pauses. The Judge declares in a voice to be reckoned with, "Not Guilty! The Innocent One has taken her sentencing and paid it in full. Case dismissed."

"What? This can't be happening! I don't understand. I'm the one who did every one of those things on the Accuser's list. He wasn't lying. He was telling the truth. I am guilty."

Stunned into silence and disbelief, you slowly walk out of the room. As you exit in numbness and confusion, someone hands you new papers. Boldly written across them in crimson are the words...NOT GUILTY.

Looking in God's Mirror

You may not believe this, but there is more! I know, I'm still trying to grasp the overwhelming act of grace that is captured in the words of a favorite hymn...that *"Thou my King should die for me."*[2] Yes, I'm shaking my head at the humbling reality too. There is more than you and I being utterly needy, completely helpless, and thoroughly sinful, and God the Judge declaring us "Not Guilty" on the basis of the blood of Jesus Christ. In addition to paying our debt in full, there is what He has given us. There is righteousness that has been credited to us as Christ-Followers!

Using Romans 4:3-6 and 5:18, rejoice as you explain your new righteousness in Christ.

Define *imputed*. (Romans 4:22 in the King James Version reads that "and therefore it was imputed to him for righteousness.")

Listen carefully to this truth: Jesus Christ's lifelong record of perfect obedience to God gets "credited" to your account when you trust in Him and are justified by God. God provides His righteousness to you, not on the basis of you keeping any moral law, but on the basis of your faith in Him.

A woman was asked one day what it felt like to be saved and she replied, "It feels as though I am standing in Jesus' shoes and He is standing in mine."

New Paperwork

Trying to comprehend this new freedom from death and having your court records completely expunged, you are still in a daze. Without even realizing you are taking steps towards the exit of the courthouse, you are shaken back into consciousness when the file clerk yells at you to stop and come to the window. "You can't leave until we have finished your paperwork Miss." As you approach the window, you have no idea what to expect. She asks for all your old records and you hand them to her out of obedience. But you let out a scream when she begins to shred all of it. "Wait! You can't do that! That's my proof that I am not guilty!" She smiles and tells you to calm down because you obviously don't understand. Before you can ask your next question, she hands you a new file with your name upon it and informs you that your name is permanently on file in the great Book of Life. It can never be altered.

As you make your way down the stairs of the building, you suddenly remember you are holding this new file in your hand and your curiosity kicks back into gear. As you open it, you stare in disbelief...you think to yourself "this can't be--this doesn't make sense." Silence. Deep breathing and even deeper wonder. And then it dawns on you: it will never make sense. Recorded in your file and credited to you is the Innocent One's life--His standing at the right hand of the Father.

Two Sides of the Coin

To understand that you are a justified sinner is to understand that there are two distinctive sides of the same coin--one side is our undeserved, thorough forgiveness and the other side is our attainment of Christ's righteousness.

"On the cross, God treats Jesus as if He had lived your life so that He can treat you as if you had lived His life." - John MacArthur, Pastor and Teacher

Looking in Your Mirror

One of the most beautiful fruits of these truths is that we can live with a confident humility because justified saints identify with others. The playing ground has all been leveled and no one has anything to boast of or boast in, except in Jesus Christ Himself.

I have had the privilege of meeting and serving Susie Buselle, a woman I will never forget. Would you like to know why? She was one of the most refreshing and challenging justified sinners I have ever met. She came out of a very rough background that included addictions and the choices that accompanied them, but she was a breath of fresh air when she walked in the room. You have never met a more humble woman because she never forgot what she was "saved from." She was confidently excited about her Savior's forgiveness like it just happened a moment ago, and she had such a hunger to know her God that called her righteous. Her life and her attitude taught me lessons that I try to live by to this day.

Which is harder for you to believe: that you are completely forgiven or that you have the righteousness of Christ? And, why?

Who in your world needs to hear this Good News and understand that there is a way to be at peace with our Holy, Creator God?

Last Look in the Mirror

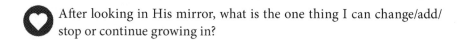 In light of being a justified sinner, ask yourself the following:

What stands out to you about God and His character today?

What is the one thing that you learned about yourself today?

How do these answers relate to your present life? What could they be saying to your mind, emotions, or will?

After looking in His mirror, what is the one thing I can change/add/ stop or continue growing in?

---

1   David Platt, *Radical, page 32.*

2   Charles Wesley, "And Can It Be," (No. 347) in *The Celebration Hymnal* (Nashville, TN;Word Entertainment Music,1997.

Act On Your Awareness--Confidence is Beautiful

My Beauty

Unique Masterpiece: Know Who You Are In God

✋ Turn off any noise and get rid of any distractions. Breathe in the quiet. Now, go to your Heavenly Father and ask Him to breathe on you His truth today.

Who is your favorite artist of all time? Did he or she ever create what is considered a masterpiece? If so, what is the name of the masterpiece?

Mas·ter·piece - Noun/´mas tər pēs/ 1. A work done with extraordinary skill; especially: a supreme intellectual or artistic achievement 2. A piece of work presented to a medieval guild as evidence of qualification for the rank of master [1]

If a group of art students were asked to describe the difference between a piece of art and a masterpiece, here is what a few might say:

> *"You can walk away from art, but you can't walk away from a Masterpiece unaffected."*

> *"A Masterpiece actually expands your consciousness."*

> *"When you see art, you see art. When you see a Masterpiece, it takes your breath away."*

> *"A Masterpiece creates its own reality. It immediately and powerfully takes you to another world."*

In today's study, my prayer is that you are going to walk away knowing that *you* are God's Masterpiece...not just an ordinary piece of art. You are one of His best and one of His most beautiful. He created you with the power to take another's breath away and He doesn't want anybody to know you without being affected by you. You were created to bring glory to the Artist.

Looking in God's Mirror

 Let's enter His most beautiful studio of truth.

What was the difference in God's reaction when He saw the beauty of earth created and then He saw the beauty of Adam and Eve created? Genesis 1:1,4,10,12,18,21,25-31

You were created in God's image and it was very good. You are more beautiful to Him than Mt. Rainier, or Victoria Falls, or the Grand Canyon. You are prettier to Him than a sunrise, or a sunset, or a rainbow in the blue sky. You are fairer than an English rose, or fresh fallen snow, or a ray of light coming through the clouds. And ladies, those works of art are unbelievably gorgeous; each one possesses the ability to captivate. But, you are the crown of His creation. You are His Masterpiece.

Read Psalms 139:1-18 and list the truths from this passage that make you feel like a Divine designer original.

Take a moment to re-read verse 14 and really focus on all that God is implying to you. Sometimes to grasp something even fuller, you need to look at its exact opposite meaning. So, write out verse 14 with the exact opposite intent of what God was saying to you. (For example: "You have evolved and you are pure junk!")

These verses scream to me that our God is a God of the individual. He creates uniquely and He knows each one intimately. No two snowflakes are alike and no two women are alike--not even twins. Various medical studies have been done and concluded that before a child's environment could shape the child, that child was already a unique individual. A child arrives with a basic make-up that determines how she will relate to the world outside of the womb.

This is no surprise to any of us who follow Christ and have read Psalms 139. The real surprise lies in the fact that we can believe this for others but we deeply struggle to believe this for ourselves. Somehow we can't grasp that I am not a product of mass production. I am not inferior to other women. I have been given both strengths and weaknesses that are solely my own. I have my unique personality that God created within me for the highest purpose of bringing Him glory.

In Isaiah 43:7, God is speaking of His sons and daughters when He tells us what we were created for. What is it?

So, let's think about this. How could your strengths bring God glory? 1 Peter 4:10-11, Ephesians 4:11-13

How could your weaknesses be the very vehicle to bring God glory? John 9:1-3, 2 Corinthians 12:7-10

God wired you in a way like no other and He considers you His greatest piece of work. With your original design, there is no one else on this earth that can bring God Almighty glory in quite the same way that you can.

This is true beauty.

My Journey from Ugly to Beautiful

Most of us are familiar with the story of the Ugly Duckling and many of us have felt like we've lived the starring role--I know I have. I was the homely bird born in a barnyard where I was teased for being flat-chested for so long. I wandered sadly from the barnyard looking for acceptance somewhere. I wondered if my hair would ever look as pretty as the girls who had long, straight hair. Would my face ever stop breaking out--why couldn't I have clear skin like so many others do? I spent many cold winters in different places never feeling like I was part of the flock. Reaching a hopeless point of thinking my life would always be a place of solitude, I was ready to throw myself away. Then I looked into the Living Water and saw the clearest reflection I had ever seen--not an ugly duckling, but a swan. I was created to be exactly who I am...a beautiful bird.

Little girls twirl in front of their daddies while holding their dress out to the side asking the question, "Aren't I pretty daddy?" Teenage girls skillfully apply their make-up and walk into their classroom hoping everybody else thinks they're looking great. Young women walk down the aisle to the man of their dreams praying he will make his bride feel beautiful for the rest of her life. The deep longing for beauty--it is within the soul of every woman ever born.

Ladies, you are being raised in a culture that wants each of you to buy into a million lies about what beauty is--an unrealistic, air-brushed body and face that is Hollywood's definition of beauty. It is chasing after a fantasy and the only ones thriving are the fashion, cosmetic, and plastic surgery industries.

The truth is that God is the only authority that has the right to define you and He declares you beautifully, fearfully, and wonderfully made.

Beauty is your uniqueness crafted by the Ultimate Artist.

Looking in Your Mirror

Name your top 5 strengths.

Name your 3 greatest weaknesses.

Choose 3 of your strengths and imagine a crazy or unlikely way each of those could be used for God's glory.

How do you think God could use each of your weaknesses to draw you closer to Him?

Where are you on this continuum with your belief?

I am garbage _____I am a masterpiece
I am ordinary _____I am one-of-a-kind

Why does it matter what you believe about yourself?

Write your own definition of beauty.

What will it take for you to believe you are beautiful?

Last Look in the Mirror

In light of being God's unique masterpiece, ask yourself the following:

What stands out to you about God and His character today?

What is the one thing that you learned about yourself today?

How do these answers relate to your present life? What could they be saying to your mind, emotions, or will?

 After looking in His mirror, what is one thing I can change/add/stop or continue growing in?

¹   "Masterpiece." *Merriam-Webster.com*. Merriam-Webster, n.d. Web. 12 Oct. 2013. <http://www.merriam-webster.com/dictionary/masterpiece>.

Act on Your Awareness--Confidence is Beautiful

My Wedding

Bride Awaiting Her Groom: Know Who You Are In God

 You have received a most formal invitation today. Break the seal and read the words from your Bridegroom.

"Dear Sweetheart,
Intimacy awaits you today as you come aside to dialogue and learn from your Lord."

In my first year of college, I began a journal and it had its own bridal section. I cut out pictures from magazines of any wedding gowns that I loved or even if the dress had just one aspect that I was crazy about--these sleeves, this lace, this beadwork, this train, etc. I also began making a list of what I wanted in my future husband--I had a list of "Must Have's" and I had a list of "It Would Be Great If's." For instance, he must be crazy in love with God, a leader with integrity, and have a blast laughing through life. Then, of course, it would be really cool if he was taller than 6 foot, loved to work out, and could play the piano or guitar in order to sing the songs of love that he had written and composed for me.

Every girl dreams about her wedding day and the groom she is going to meet at the end of the aisle.

Your Wedding Dreams Today

If you were putting a journal together today with your very own bridal section, how would you fill in these blanks?

My Gown Would Look Like:

My Colors Would Be:

The Ceremony Would Take Place:

One of My Dreams

Let me take you back to my teenage bedroom in Fairfield, California. It was a room full of soft pinks and blues surrounded by an antique brass bed, beautiful old rocking chair, darkly stained chest, and dark mirrored vanity. There I am seated on my rose taffeta stool looking into the mirror with tears leaving streaks in my makeup as they run down my face. I realize that my outward appearance mirrors my soul--dark, ugly, and empty.

The door to my room opens slowly and it's almost as if sunlight streams in behind him. I can't help but turn towards it and him. "Oh no! Not him!" But as he walks over slowly, I am made aware of my disheveled state, and I don't want anybody to see me like this. I feel so ashamed that, at this moment, I literally hate myself. I turn away from the mirror.

"Christie," he says. I interrupt him quickly so he doesn't waste his time, "Trust me. You don't want anything to do with me." He steadily approaches me and takes my face in his hands. It feels so intimate that I am a million shades of red and feel utterly exposed and vulnerable. His thumb wipes my tears away and as he reaches towards my hair, I see my make-up smeared all over his hands... now they're black! How humiliating! My filth all over him...but what's that he put on my head? Probably a dunce hat for all my stupid choices. He senses my question, takes my hand, and moves me towards my mirror again.

I don't want to see my disgraced self that close up. "Please. Can't we stop this?" He gently insists and I catch a glimpse. "What!? What is going on?!" I'm dumbfounded. I cannot stop staring. It's like time stood still and I am looking at the reflection of a young woman with a completely clean face, fresh with new makeup. She has bright, clear eyes, no longer swollen, red, and puffy. And, of all things, there is a crown sitting upon her head. That's what he put on me...a crown with a veil flowing from the golden rim to my shoulders. And what's more, I am dressed in the most beautiful white gown imaginable.

His voice sounds like a declaration as he says, "You are my beautiful bride, pure and undefiled!"

Looking in God's Mirror

God's Word will be a full-length mirror today, reflecting you as a bride-in-waiting. Keep your spiritual eyes open. Don't miss a thing.

You are His Chosen Bride (and it's not a dream!)

If you are a Christ-follower, then you are now the bride of Christ Jesus, whom He loves and has chosen to bestow upon a crown of beauty. The God of the Universe has chosen you. The significance of being chosen reflects how treasured you truly are, as well as how you should see yourself.

Read Isaiah 61:10 - meditate on it - then describe yourself based on this verse.

Read Isaiah 61:3 where it states the ministry of the Messiah.

"And provide for those who grieve in Zion--
to bestow on them a crown of beauty instead of ashes,
the oil of gladness instead of mourning,
and a garment of praise instead of a spirit of despair.
They will be called oaks of righteousness,
a planting of the LORD for the display of his splendor."

Jesus wants you to live like you are a bride with a beautiful crown instead of a mourner covered in ashes. Yet so many times we live covered in the ashes of our sin. You know what the ashes feel like don't you? The ashes are the private sins we mourn--the things we've said and done that nobody knows about and we would be terrified if anybody did know. The sins you cry about when it's late at night and you are all alone. The sins that make you feel ugly, feel empty, and feel like hiding. What does God have to say about the ashes? We will get to that in just a minute.

Before we do, privately (not to be shared) name and confess your ashes.

The *"crown of beauty"* that Isaiah talks about is an elaborate, ornamental headdress, much like a regal crown with a wedding veil. In ancient days, this headdress identified a woman as both bride and queen. So this portrait is one of God blowing away the ashes and replacing them with a crown identifying each of us as the Bride of the King. That's how God sees you...His beautiful bride!

Satan, our enemy, knows exactly who we are, but he wants us to see ourselves as constantly covered in a heap of ashes because he knows that we will act like who we think we are. We will live out who we believe ourselves to be.

Now back to my question earlier--what does God have to say about the ashes?

In Matthew 5:4 God teaches us that *"blessed are those who mourn (their sins), for they shall be comforted."*

In 2 Corinthians 7:10 God says, *"For the sorrow that is according to the will of God produces a repentance without regret, leading to salvation; but the sorrow of the world produces death."*

God revealed an amazing truth to me one day tucked within this Corinthian verse: Guilt is from God and Shame is from Satan, and there is a huge difference between the two.

Godly Sorrow is from God:	**Shame is from Satan:**
- Godly sorrow is healthy	- Shame is unhealthy
- Focuses me on the will of God	- Distracts me from God's will

- My eyes are focused on Jesus	- My eyes are focused on me
- Purpose: leads me to repentance	- Purpose: keeps me in whirlpool of self-focus
- Cries "I need You"	- Immobilizes and silences
- Enables me to move forward	- Stagnant, I cannot move anywhere

God calls us to recognize the ashes of sin, mourn our rebellion against a Holy God, and seek repentance to walk forward in newness of being His Bride awaiting our Bridegroom. So Jesus came that the ashes might be replaced with a crown of beauty--hallelujah!

Ladies, take that previous list of ashes and take the time right now to allow that guilt to send you to the foot of the cross where you will find forgiveness.

1 John 1:9 reminds us that "*if we confess our sins, He is faithful and just and will forgive us our sins and purify us from all unrighteousness.*"

Each day you awake with a choice: the choice to see yourself as a bride wearing a crown of beauty or as a mourner wearing ashes.

Don't buy into the **lie** of living in the ash pile.
Cling to the **truth** that you are His chosen beautiful Bride!

Your Bridegroom loves you. You need to hear that loud and clear. Do you?

Now for some cultural background--You need to understand some history behind the Jewish weddings of old to really see the fullness of Jesus Christ's love for you. There are three very distinct parts to the Jewish wedding ceremony, and each one represents an aspect of our relationship to our Lord.

1: The Contract   This was the legal agreement.

A contract between two sets of parents would be negotiated and, as a result, the dowry would be determined upon their economic status and the estimated value of the girl. The "Bride Price" could be very steep, even comparable to the price of a new house today. Then, when the dowry was paid, there was a ceremony in which the couple was betrothed. This part of the ceremony symbolized a permanent commitment.

How do you see this commitment between Jesus Christ and His bride in Ephesians 5:25-27?

Do you see what a "high bride price" you and I cost our Redeemer? Yet, like the Jewish ritual, Jesus has taken care of our legal contract. He paid the dowry of God's wrath against sin in full with His precious blood, in order that each one of us can be his bride.

2: The Betrothal Year   This was the time of preparation.

Next, the groom went away in order to add a room to his father's house. It usually took about a year, but the actual time was determined by the father. During this time of separation, the bride would prepare her gown. It involved much time and patience and included many intricate details.

According to Matthew 25:1-13, what can you glean about this time of preparation?

Based on John 14:1-4, how does Jesus, as our Bridegroom, use this time of preparation?

Can you even imagine what your dwelling will be like? But, as we wait for His arrival, we have our own things to prepare. We need to choose what our wedding gown is going to look like for our big day. We do this with our choices to obey or disobey each and every day.

3: The Wedding Day   This was the final celebration and culmination of the relationship.

After the groom had completed their new house, he came to the bride's house, got the bride, and took her to the father's house for the actual wedding and wedding feast. It was always a surprise when it occurred.

Glean truths from Revelation 19:6-9 about your future wedding day.

The Groom returns for His bride whom He loves and the greatest celebration of all begins in eternity! We don't know the day or time, but we can be assured He will return.

Looking in Your Mirror

What do you want to be wearing when your groom, Jesus, returns for you? How beautifully elaborate will your dress be? How much time will you have spent making yourself ready for His appearance?

In Revelation 19:7 it says, "...*the bride made herself ready.*" Note the verb tense. In other words, we cannot get ready when we hear the trumpet call and know He has come to get us. It will be too late. We must prepare ourselves now!

How, you ask?

I know that I never wanted to look more breathtaking than I did on my wedding day for Mark. My thoughts were consumed with how he would view me when he saw me for the first time walking down the aisle in my beaded, white gown and veil. What thoughts would cross his mind? Would he catch his breath or would his heart skip a beat? That's what I was hoping.

Your wedding day to Jesus Christ is coming! Your thoughts and my thoughts should be consumed with looking our most gorgeous for our Groom on that day. "Fine linen" in Revelation 19:8 refers to the righteous acts of the saints. So we clothe ourselves with our choices to obey and express love towards our Savior. How pretty will you be that day?

Don't buy into the **lie** that the Bridegroom isn't coming back for you, so there's no use getting ready. You've always got someday!

Cling to the **truth** that since you will never know the time of His return, you are to be ready this very moment!

Last Look in the Mirror

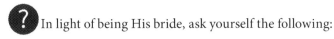 In light of being His bride, ask yourself the following:

What stands out to you about God and His character today?

What is the one thing that you learned about yourself today?

How do these answers relate to your present life? What could they be saying to your mind, emotions, or will?

 After looking in His mirror, what is the one thing I can change/add/ stop or continue growing in?

Act On Your Awareness--Confidence is Beautiful

My Security

Citizen of Heaven: Know Who You Are In God

✋ Thank you for stepping away from your busyness and making God's Word a priority in your life. Ask Him to give you an unexpected blessing today.

In the 8th grade, many teens have the opportunity to learn about US history up close and personal with a trip to Washington, DC and New York through their schools. When the chance for my daughter arrived, we chose not to go with the school, but instead to take advantage of this becoming our second major mother/daughter trip and travel to the East Coast ourselves...and we had such a blast!

When we toured Ellis Island, neither of us were prepared for it to be so fascinating or for the realization of how many people wanted to leave their home country in order to become an American citizen. It wasn't that easy or cheap! Inspectors questioned arrivals about their admissibility, and if they were not pleased with their answers or feel they didn't have the proper written records on hand, they were denied and awaited deportation, or they were detained and put under the prison-like care of detention guards and matrons. Military surgeons performed ten-second medical examinations of each prospective citizen, using chalk to write on their clothing any medical condition that the person was flagged for. Many did not get into the country due to their health condition after crossing the Atlantic. Often, aliens were excluded because they lacked funds or had no friends or relatives nearby. Citizenship was not a guarantee by any means. It was a very coveted commodity.

Citizenship was extremely important to the New Testament Philippians too. The Romans would settle retired army veterans in different parts of the Empire and then those colonies would model their city government after Rome. These settlements would take their privileges and duties as Roman citizens extremely seriously with great patriotism and pride. Philippi was just such a settlement.

Just as Philippi was a colony of Rome on foreign soil, so the Church (you and I) is a colony of heaven on foreign soil, Earth.

Philippians 3:20 "... *for our citizenship is in heaven ...*"

Salvation gave you and I citizenship to heaven--no crossing the Atlantic, needing proof of belonging through documents, having to be medically examined, or verifying that we have enough money. The moment you and I responded to God, picked up our cross, and began to follow Him, we were given new citizenship--citizenship in heaven!

Looking in God's Mirror

 Look at what He desires to reveal to you today. He wants it crystal clear in your mind and your heart.

What does Revelation 21:1-8, 22-26 teach you about God's proof that you are a citizen of heaven?

Write out Luke 10:20.

The Greek verb "written" in Luke 10:20 means that it stands written and was once-for-all written. How does that build security in your heart?

Knowing that you are a citizen of heaven, what does Hebrews 11:13 call you while you dwell here on earth? _____ & _____

Meditate on the implications these verses have on you and your life.

There's No Place Like Home

If you could have a ticket to vacation anywhere on this planet, what would be your first choice? Why?

I have a favorite place--it's the Abaco Islands in the Bahamas. My husband and I have been there four times so far, and it is still our number one choice for a vacation. I love everything about island life, especially the pace because it is absolutely opposite of how I live day to day. I love the warm, friendly Bahamian people. I love the friends that we travel with--we have laughed till we cried, we have crammed a million memories into each visit, and we've got each other's backs looking for sharks while we snorkel. I love the beauty of the white sand beaches and clearest turquoise water you've ever seen. I love eating the conch fritters and fresh dolphin fish and Vern's daily baked key lime pie. I love going out every day in our boat and playing in the water. I could go on and on and on...but even with all those 'loves,' there is still something about *going home.*

There is just something about your own home. You are on the plane and all you can think about is getting back to your kids, your bed, your pillow, your kitchen, your bathroom, and your things. Dorothy was right when she said, *"There's no place like home!"*

Girls, heaven is your home. We are just "on vacation" down here; we are just pilgrims passing through. We are getting on a plane, and we are going to fly home one day. And when we get there, I promise you, we'll be clicking our heels and saying with tears in our eyes, *"There's no place like home!"*

Another Look in God's Mirror

Abraham proved his belief by living as a "stranger" just passing through. How did his life scream that his home was not on this earth? Hebrews 11:8-12

Abraham lived as an alien in the land of promise dwelling in *tents* because he was looking for the "city"--heaven itself. By living in the canvas-like tent, he was daily reminded of how temporary this earthly life is, that it is not a place to get too settled into.

We, too, are given our temporal *tents*--our bodies. Each time our *tent* gets sick, injured, grows older, develops a handicap, or carries a disease, it is a clear reminder that it wasn't created to last forever. I believe it is supposed to be a clear prompting that we are not home and this is not the place to sink down our roots. (Abraham is very lucky his tent didn't wrinkle, sag, or leak!)

The apostle Paul challenges us over and over to be spiritually minded and not to get so wrapped up in the "here and now."

What do you hear him saying to your heart in these passages?

Colossians 3:1-3

Philippians 3:12-14

Matthew 16: 22-27

Think about whether your life fulfills these truths or falls short.

It is so easy to get wrapped up in this life on earth--the drama of girlfriends, keeping up with all your texts, trying to build relationships, your family plans for the weekend, working out, deciding what to wear in the morning, going to work, and the list goes on. We lose perspective. We get things all turned around. We start thinking this is *home*.

Walking in Another's Shoes

One Pair of Shoes

A Diary Entry - November 1859

I jes want to runs away to escape my pain, my everlasting bondage and torment day after day. I wants to runs towards the North star because that's what I wad told to do. I wants to runs till I find freedom. I wants to live in a house wheres theres no lashing--no screaming--no being used for sex and tossed back outside. I don't wants my babies to have to work this hard and haves nuttin to show fer it. Wez too young to have this much pain and all this hate sirrin in my tummy. Theres gots to be more than this life. Theres gots to be more.

Clotee, slave teen girl - Belmont Plantation, Virginia [1]

I find it very convicting that *Cleote* holds tighter to her heavenly citizenship than I do. The American slaves of the South suffered atrocities that we cannot imagine, and yet because of that very suffering, it was crystal clear to them that this was not a place to get attached to--this wasn't home.

The negro spirituals are some of the most moving songs ever written, and not to my surprise, heaven was a recurring theme. Listen in....

"Going home in the chariot in the morning"
"Until I reach-a ma home, I nevah inten' to give de journey ovah"
"Lord, I'm bearing heavy burdens tryin' to get home"
"I want to go home in the morning..." [2]

Another Pair of Shoes - July 2001

Sreypov Chan, a young Cambodian woman, has a recurring dream of being chased by gangsters. After running till she could no longer, she's caught and thrown into a disease-filled, cockroach-infested room. In terror, she knows what will happen next. She will be whipped with metal cables, shocked with a loose electrical wire, locked inside of a cage, and then gang raped. This dream is Srepyov's reality.

At the tender age of seven, an age when most girls are going to birthday parties, she was being sold to work as a sex slave in a brothel. Her mother was the one who made the sale.

"For years, pimps forced Sreypov to have sex with as many as 20 men a day. If she didn't meet her quota, or if she tried to run away, she was punished in unthinkable ways--burned with a hot poker, covered with biting insects, and worse. "I wanted to die," she says." [3]

Again, when life is hard, when life is horrible, the reality that this life here on earth is not the grandest or most glorious thing ever hits you in the face. Maybe we're living like this earth is our home because our lives are too easy? Too comfortable? Too luxurious?

Looking in Your Mirror

Place an 'X' on this scale where you are at today.

Feet Deeply Planted On Earth   Anticipating Heaven

What factors are contributing to where you are at on the scale?

Draw a star where would you like to be on the scale.

What changes need to be made in order for you to move towards the star?

How would believing that you are an alien here with a home being built in heaven give you more security?

Write a short poem or chorus or catch phrase that you could repeat over and over to remind yourself that you aren't home yet.

Last Look in the Mirror

 In light of being a citizen of heaven, ask yourself the following:

What stands out to you about God and His character today?

What is the one thing that you learned about yourself today?

How do these answers relate to your present life? What could they be saying to your mind, emotions, or will?

 After looking in His mirror, what is the one thing I can change/add/ stop or continue growing in?

[1]   Patrick C. McKissack, *A Picture of Freedom: The Diary of Clotee, a Slave Girl* (New York: Scholastic, Inc., 1997) pp. 103-117.

[2]   "Between 1865 and 1925." *Song Official Site of Negro Spirituals, Antique Gospel Music.* Spiritual Workshop, Paris, n.d. Web. 12 Oct. 2013.
[3]   Stop Modern Slavery. "Nightmare Come Alive." Hope For Slaves. Wordpress, 04 2012. Web. 11 Dec 2012. <http://hopeforslaves.com/category/may-day/>.

WRAP UP TO YOUR SECOND WEEK OF STUDY

I'm raising my crystal glass of sparkling apple cider to you in a toast right now--please join me.

"Here is to you becoming a confident young woman. My wish for you is to always be aware of who you are and to know yourself well. I long for you to taste the beginning of a lifelong hunger to get to know your God and His heart. And may you stand strong in your true identity--who you are in Jesus Christ. You are His princess. You are justified through His blood. You are His masterpiece. You are His bride. You are Heaven's citizen."

Confidence is awareness of who you are, who God is, and who you are in God. Act on your awareness because confidence is beautiful!

As You Start Your Third Week of Study

Imagine yourself living day in and day out in a wasteland. You spend each moment in a world full of garbage, void of color, dry and ugly, with little to no vegetation. As lifeless as the land is, you are surrounded by throngs of people wandering around restlessly as if they are zombies searching for something.

Now imagine yourself living every day in a flourishing, vegetative landscape. The people are few and far between, but the look of joy on each face is not one you'll soon forget. You are overwhelmed with the abundance of greenery and how lush it is. Vibrant colors surround you at every turn.

This is the difference between the land of bondage and the land of freedom.

Where do you want to spend your life? I promise you this…freedom is worth fighting for.

Soften your spirit and listen closely as the Holy Spirit speaks to you this week.

FREEDOM IS WORTH FIGHTING FOR

DAY 11: My Baggage
Why is it important not to live in the land of the past? Are you still carrying baggage around?

DAY 12: My Self-Righteousness
How harmful is it to live in the land of obligation? How self-righteous have you become?

DAY 13: My Fears
How do you move out of the land of "what if?" How can you become a brave woman?

DAY 14: My Worries
Why do you choose to live in the land of anxiety? Can Paul teach you how to get rid of worry?

DAY 15: My Strongholds (part one)
Have you unknowingly moved into the land of spiritual bondage? How can you break free from your chains?

Freedom is Worth Fighting For

My Baggage

Living in the Land of the Past:
Freedom from the Captivity of Sin

Today's study needs your full attention and your eyes wide open. Ask the Holy Spirit to reveal to you the baggage you are still carrying around from your past. Ask Him to make it incredibly clear how much freer you will be without it. Thank Him in advance for this journey of freedom.

Packed Baggage?

I couldn't believe it! Every time I held up my left hand, there was an engagement ring staring back at me! I was officially a fiancée...a betrothed woman... engaged and counting the days till the wedding. Between the stars in my eyes and my strategic, diligent planning for eight months, I had no idea that I was going to walk down the aisle with some huge suitcases attached to my soul that I had never unpacked.

Although my luggage ensemble looked high-end and quite impressive, each piece had its own story and its own burdens that came along with it.

One of my bags was full of unrealistic expectations for this new marriage relationship. In my grandparents I had a role model for commitment, but nowhere in my circle of life could I find a strong example of a faithful and growing marriage founded on Jesus Christ. Growing up, I was most impacted by the choices of adultery, divorce, living together, and unhealthy dating. So, by the time I had become a Christ-follower and went off to Bible college, I had romanticized and fantasized the ideal marriage to the point that I was completely set up for disappointment and hurt.

I thought marriage would be a man and a woman willingly sharing their hearts and souls and spirits, always wanting to hold hands or touch each other, freely giving and receiving intimacy, anticipating time in the Word together, praying every night as they lay in bed, always wanting to build each other up and challenge each other to use their gifts, and determined to turn this world upside down for Christ. I naively thought that I would be able to meet every one of his needs and that he would live to meet every one of my needs. And actually, the list goes on.

There was no way Mark or any human could live out my unrealistic dreams and expectations.

I had some baggage that needed to be unpacked or our marriage was in serious trouble!

Unpacked Baggage?

I think I thought that by getting on a train and going to another country for college that I would somehow be able to leave my bitterness and anger towards my mother behind me...wrong! There is no such thing as running away or going far enough away from a person to erase the pain that has been caused. I had a choice--keep trying to ignore it or deal with it once and for all. As I began this exciting new stage of life, I realized that I wanted to be free from my past. So I pulled out my suitcase of pain and disappointment and began unpacking it.

I started with asking God to help me purge myself of this poison called resentment. I cried out, "Just show me how to let it go, Abba!" He gently whispered back in response, "It begins with forgiveness." So I got out my journal and began writing down all the ways I had been hurt or let down by my mom because I needed to give words and pictures to my pain. Then a wise person challenged me to stop judging her according to God's Word; I couldn't hold her to a standard she didn't know existed. That enabled me to start seeing life through her eyes. I didn't excuse her choices, but I began to understand that they weren't quite as clear cut as I made them out to be. Leaning wholly on the Holy Spirit, I asked for the willingness to forgive her for my own healing and my own freedom to be able to move on.

It is humbling to share with someone that you have held onto unhealthy emotions for far too long and that you want to forgive them. But it was even more humbling and frightening to admit that it only hurt so much because I have always desired to be close to her. Fear of rejection can be a powerful thing, but my desire for freedom finally won out.

One more piece of emotional luggage unpacked--thank you Lord.

Let's Talk Baggage for a Bit

Bag·gage – Noun / bag-ij / 1 intangible things (as feelings, circumstances, or beliefs) that get in the way [1]

Dr. Les Parrott and Dr. Neil Clark Warren provide a compelling definition of emotional baggage: "History is what has happened in our lives. Baggage is how we feel about it. Your psychological perspective on your past determines, to a great extent, your personal health and vitality." [2]

God is very concerned about your life and your vitality.

What does He want for you in Galatians 5:13? What does He call you to?

Ladies, unpacked baggage keeps you from being free, and I am here to tell you that freedom is worth fighting for! Dr. Parrott and Dr. Warren continue, "Everyone has a history and an emotional response to it. What matters, when it comes to being a healthy, thriving human being, is whether or not you have deliberately unpacked your baggage. If not, it is bound to thwart your personal growth. You can never feel profoundly significant at your core until you make peace with this emotional baggage." [3]

You find yourself bound by inner vows you made to yourself growing up, yet these are usually unrealistic and extreme. You find yourself holding tightly to bitterness because forgiveness seems impossible at this point. Unpacked baggage keeps you emotionally and spiritually immature...for the rest of your life if left alone.

Doctors Parrott and Warren conclude, "The healthiest among us have rummaged around in the contents of their own suitcases. They have explored what they feel and why they feel the way they do about their history. This act of simply identifying and labeling their emotions as they explore their past serves as an amazing springboard to personal growth, self-insight and maturity. It even impacts physical well-being...In order to get beyond your past; you sometimes need to get into your past." [4]

How does God teach you to deal with your baggage from the past and the impact that it is having on your present? His truth applied can set you free from it.

FREEDOM IS WORTH FIGHTING FOR!
"You, my sisters, were called to be free." Galatians 5:13

How Do We Fight The Accumulated Suitcases?

Ask God for His healing help. He invites you to cast your cares upon Him (1 Peter 5:7).

Take inventory of your luggage.

Use this list of possible suitcases to identify baggage you carry in your life. Underline any that apply to you. Then go back through and circle any that you have yet to process and unpack.

Unsure of parent's love

Felt neglected or ignored by a parent

Favoritism amongst siblings

Divorce of parents

Custody battles

Raised with step or half siblings

Alcoholic parent

Drug addicted parent

Emotionally/Verbally abusive parent/relative

Physically abusive parent/relative

Emotionally/Verbally abusive sibling

Physically abusive sibling

Emotionally/Verbally abusive boyfriend or close friend

Physically abusive boyfriend

Raped/sexual abuse

Legalistic home

Parents highly concerned about their image/image of family

Pressure of high parental
expectations
Anorexia/bulimia
Parents in Pastoral ministry
Parents served as Field Missionaries
Mental illness in family
Chronic illness in family
Molestation/sexual abuse
Early sexual encounters
Pornography
Financial stress in home
Parent out of work for
extended period of time
Use of alcohol
Use of drugs
Adopted
Unplanned pregnancy
Abortion
Suicidal attempt
Death of parent
Death of significant person
Foster home

Parent had affair
Learning disability
Physical disability
Serious accident
Bullied
Criminal behavior
Ran away from home
Manipulated by parents/others
Hypocrisy in home
Depression
Rejected by sibling, step-parent
Academic struggles/pressures
Betrayal by friends
Military family/moving around
Single parent home
Suicide by a family member
Family revolved around
kids and their schedules
Spoiled materialistically
Enmeshment with one of your
parents/parent overly attached
to you out of their loneliness

Discover your unhealthy behavior & reactions

In the last year, which of these behaviors do you find yourself repeating over and over? Which of these actions do others accuse you of? Be honest with yourself and circle any that apply to you.

Withdraw from others
Silent over hurt
Hard time sleeping
Hard time eating
Over eating and/or binge eating
Fearful
Defensive
Cry easily
Self-pity
Angry
Frustrated
Easily Irritated

Highly Sensitive
Blaming others
Critical
Judgmental
No need for others/do it myself
Throwing fits
Don't say "I'm sorry"
Denial
Doubt God
Angry at God
Distant from God
Hopeless

Anxious
Manipulate others
Threaten others
Can't forgive
Can't stop thinking about something
Controlling
Apologize for everything
Can't say 'no'
Need to please people
No desire to be close to people
Using alcohol to escape
Using drugs to forget
Impatient
Unsatisfied
Constantly need more
Must be busy
Uncomfortable with quiet
Argumentative
Arrogant

Complaining
Compromising
Lying
Defiant
Insulate self emotionally
Not able to trust others
Justify
Laugh it off
Minimize things
Ridicule others
Threaten
Violent
Hypocritical living
Need to win
Need to be your idea of perfect
Hard on self
Sense of entitlement
Cling to rights

Now take your unhealthy behaviors and see if you can connect each one to any piece of unpacked baggage. One suitcase may have several behaviors coming out of it and some behaviors may be packed in several suitcases. Take your time--your freedom is worth fighting for.

Since these unhealthy behaviors can be blind spots in your life, ask a trusted friend who knows you well to give you feedback too.

Be ready to share one suitcase that needs to be unpacked and one childish behavior.

Realize you are influenced by your baggage but not defined by it.

Each person's past is a unique combination of positive elements and negative elements. We even see this in the life and lineage of Jesus Christ. Recall our Savior's heritage: David commits murder and adultery (2 Samuel 11:1-27), Rahab practices prostitution (Joshua 2:1-7), and there are no words capable of describing Mannaseh's evil (2 Chronicles 33:1-17). On the other hand, Abraham's deep faith leads him to a mountain with Isaac (Genesis 22:1-19), Solomon has everything this world has to offer and asks for wisdom (1 Kings 3:9-10), and Mary bows her fear and lack of understanding to a God who knows best (Luke 1:38). You need to see and believe that your past, with all of its positives and all of its negatives, does not define who you choose to be. You are influenced by your history, but you are not defined by it.

What part of your history does NOT define you?

Many adults can still be found laying all the blame for their own lack of character at their parents' feet.

In Genesis 3:8-13, what does the Garden of Eden teach us about man's first instinct when it comes to blame?

Let's make a distinction.
Who are you responsible for? (Galatians 6:5) _____

Who are you responsible to? (Ecclesiastes 12:13-14) _____

Does God indicate whether he thinks behavior and patterns of defensiveness can be broken? Look at Isaiah 43:18-19.

Evaluate your inner vows

Inner vows are all about keeping safe. They are a false and dangerous kind of protection that are usually created in response to an event; the response may or may not have been verbalized. The nature of the inner vow is such that it takes the form of "I will never..." or "I will always..." or some other statement of our will. Inner vows may sound good on the surface, but they should always be evaluated with caution.

The distinctive mark of an inner vow is that it resists the normal maturation process. Inner vows resist change and create private pockets in our hearts that shut God out because we've already decided what will or will not be done. We do not grow out of them, and they can easily lead to the hardening of our hearts.

A "heart of stone" is a defense mechanism, a hiding place we believe will protect us from hurt, but which in fact makes us the loneliest people in the world. The Church is filled with hearts of stone; people who can superficially love and serve others, but who can't allow others to minister to them, and miss out on the freedom by which we are designed to live. Inner vows are one aspect of a stony heart. Although they are made early in life and are often forgotten, they act as directives, which control our responses to situations and people around us.

What are 2-3 inner vows you made to yourself growing up? ("I will always...," "I'll never...," "I am going to make sure...")

What does Psalms 95:8 warn you against?

What does Ezekiel 36:26 tell you about God's will for you?

Take some time to pray about your heart and any inner vows you harbor. Here are some sample prayers that might help:

> *Dear Lord, I can't remember any vows that I made as a child, but if I did, would You reveal them to me? I want to confess them and have their power in my heart broken. In Jesus's name, Amen.*
>
> *Amazing God, I want a soft heart--I really do. I know I have pockets of my heart that I don't give You access to and I want that to change now. I want to invite You into any places that have become hard and please create in me a new heart, O God. Amen.*
>
> *Loving Father, I confess that I have sinned in making the following vows: (name vows). Forgive me. In the name of Jesus, I declare they no longer have any influence over me, and I cut myself free from their effects. Protect me from the enemy and the way he tries to get into my heart. All for You, Amen.*

Forgive--Others and Self

One of the largest and heaviest suitcases we carry around is that of withholding forgiveness. It usually adds another piece of luggage filled with bitterness to our ensemble.

We have so many reasons why we can't forgive or why we shouldn't forgive:

"It would be like telling them what they did was okay."
"It won't make any difference. It doesn't change anything."
"That person needs to say they are sorry."
"My offender needs to admit that they were wrong first!"
"My anger is justified."
"Then he/she just gets away with it--there are no consequences."
"I have to get past my hurt first, and then I'll think about it."
"They don't deserve to be forgiven."
"I want to make them pay."

Hear this clearly--forgiveness doesn't excuse the sin or the one who committed it. It doesn't even demand reconciliation with someone who is either unrepentant or unsafe. It never opens you up to more abuse!

The Bible compares forgiving people to releasing them from a legal debt. So, to forgive is your choice to "write off" the debt. You decide to tear up the account and render it "canceled" because you accept the fact that you will never get back from that person what was owed you. Instead, you entrust them into the hands of a righteous Judge who promises us that He will take care of business for us. "*It is Mine to avenge,*" says the Lord (Romans 12:19). Remember that He is El Roi, the God who sees everything that happens to you, and His heart breaks for you. Each and every sin will be dealt with. God desires freedom for you and for the person who hurt you.

The truth that so many miss is that granting forgiveness is actually *your* ticket to freedom. It is your opportunity to make a choice that allows you to heal, protects you from bitterness, and it is your moment to reflect God's beauty. To choose not to forgive is like handcuffing you to the person who hurt you. It keeps you emotionally bound with them, but forgiving is the key to unlock those manacles and set you free. You have been through enough, dear ones, and you deserve every fruit the tree of freedom has to offer!

What does Colossians 3:13 and Ephesians 4:31-32 say to you about forgiveness?

Bitterness is bondage and you, my dear one, are the prisoner. Someone has said that "bitterness is like drinking poison and expecting the other person to die."

What does God warn us about bitterness in Hebrews 12:15?

PRIVATE: Is there anyone from your past that you have not forgiven yet? Why are you still angry or why does it still hurt?

Commit to grow and move forward

How does God challenge us to be free from our past?

Philippians 3:12-14

2 Peter 3:18

Last Look in the Mirror

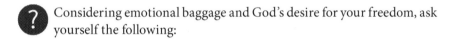 Considering emotional baggage and God's desire for your freedom, ask yourself the following:

What stands out to you about God and His character today?

What is the one thing that you learned about yourself today?

How do these answers relate to your present life? What could they be saying to your mind, emotions, or will?

With transformation as my goal, what is the one thing I can change/add/stop or continue growing in?

1   "Baggage." *Merriam-Webster.com*. Merriam-Webster, n.d. Web. 12 Oct. 2013. <http://www.merriam-webster.com/dictionary/baggage>.

2   Parrott, Dr. Les, and Neil Clark Warren. "Losing Your Emotional Baggage." Two Of Us. Pivot Concepts. Web. 11 Dec 2012. <http://www.twoofus.org/educational-content/articles/losing-your-emotional-baggage/index.asp&xgt;

3   Ibid.

4   Ibid.

5   Ibid.

Freedom Is Worth Fighting For

My Self-Righteousness

Living in the Land of Obligation: Freedom from the Captivity of Sin

This time you share with God is invaluable. The truths you are learning today have the power to impact all of your tomorrows. Don't rush these moments.

A Look in the Mirror

Be honest with yourself and answer the following questions:

When I feel I've been wronged, am I quick to assign motives as to why the other person hurt me?

     NEVER   SELDOM   USUALLY   ALWAYS

Do I find it easy to build a case against someone that makes me seem right and him/her wrong?

     NEVER   SELDOM   USUALLY   ALWAYS

Am I overly concerned about who is to blame?

NEVER SELDOM USUALLY ALWAYS

Do I ask questions with built-in assumptions?

NEVER SELDOM USUALLY ALWAYS

Do I think I am better than others around me?

NEVER SELDOM USUALLY ALWAYS

Do I tend to remove myself from people who do not agree with me?

NEVER SELDOM USUALLY ALWAYS

Do I find myself critical of others?

NEVER SELDOM USUALLY ALWAYS

Do I wear my 'godly character' like it's a badge?

NEVER SELDOM USUALLY ALWAYS

Do I believe God loves some more than others?

NEVER SELDOM USUALLY ALWAYS

Do I fear loss of approval or love?

NEVER SELDOM USUALLY ALWAYS

Do I have a hard time admitting my weaknesses?

NEVER SELDOM USUALLY ALWAYS

Do I tend be highly concerned about my image in public?

NEVER SELDOM USUALLY ALWAYS

Do I tend to serve others expecting some sort of recognition?

NEVER SELDOM USUALLY ALWAYS

Add up the total number of answers that were either 'Usually" or "Always".
_____ / 12

If you scored 6/12 or higher, you are being held captive by the sin of self-righteousness. Regardless of your score, let's take a look at this sin and how it holds us captive.

What is self-righteousness? Self-righteousness is a form of religious pride, and all pride is an inflated sense of one's personal status or accomplishments.

> **Wikpedia**: *It is a feeling of smug moral superiority derived from a sense that one's beliefs, actions, or affiliations are of greater virtue than those of the average person.* [1]
> **Webster Dictionary**: *narrow-mindedly moralistic* [2]
> **Web Definition**: *Holier-than-thou; excessively or hypocritically pious; "a sickening sanctimonious smile"* [3]

Self-righteousness is so easy to slip into, and often without even realizing it. Just as termites eat up the wood within a home, leaving the exterior looking good-as-new, so does self-righteous pride destroy one from within. Jesus pointed this out in the lives of the Pharisees when He said in Matthew 23:27, *"Woe to you... hypocrites! You are like whitewashed tombs, which look beautiful on the outside, but on the inside are full of the bones of the dead and everything unclean."* Sister, we don't want to be described this way, or, far worse, live this way. By taking a look at the ways self-righteousness takes us as its prisoner, I think we will be able to see if we have become blind to our own self-righteousness.

 God has much to say about the chains of self-righteousness and how they enslave. Study well.

When Self-Righteousness Takes You Prisoner

We find ourselves falling captive to self-centered living when we find ourselves needing to perform for God and for others. And, I know all about performing. I did it for over half my life. I grew up trying to earn my parent's love after they divorced and just carried that over into my personal mantras for life: "Am I doing enough to please You God?," "strive for perfection because that's excellence," "notice me God," "pick me Lord," and the list goes on.

How do you perform for people? What do you do to try to earn their approval?

How do you perform for God? What do you do to try to earn His approval?

What does Isaiah 64:6 say about your very best performance before God?

The need to perform is rooted in a belief that we somehow need to earn God's love and acceptance, which in essence, cuts us off from the grace of God. God's grace by definition is unmerited favor, kindness focused and given, and benevolence extended. Grace is given by God through Jesus Christ and grace is received by His children.

Search Ephesians 2:4-9 and dig out the incredible truths about the grace of God. Record them in the margin.

You cannot be performing for God and believing in His grace at the same time. Choose grace and live authentically because there is no performance that will ever be "great enough"--grace is received, not earned. The sooner you believe that, the sooner you are set free.

Another way we find ourselves falling captive to self-centered living is when we feel the need to "be good" or begin to believe that deep down we really are "good." We begin to think that if God judged according to giant scales, our "goodness" would outweigh our "badness." We can always find another person that if we compare our life choices to theirs, we feel morally superior. We are deceived with the notion that at the core of our being, we have good motives.

What does God say in Jeremiah 17:9 about our hearts, the core of our beings?

To those who were confident of their own goodness and looked down on everybody else, Jesus told a parable in Luke 18:9-14. Please read and meditate on it. What do you learn from the Pharisee and the sinner?

State in your own words what you believe to be the main truths that Jesus was teaching.

The real trouble with being good is we are tempted to think we don't need to be forgiven (well, not much anyway). And if we don't need forgiveness, then we don't need Jesus Christ or His death or His resurrection...we just need ourselves. That is terribly dangerous thinking.

We also find ourselves falling captive to self-centered living when we have the need to impress people. We will suffer from and be bound to the deception that our worth is based upon how others view us, thus we will strive to win their approval of us. We will find ourselves expending inordinate amounts of time, energy and money trying to unknowingly seduce and/or manipulate others into getting them to validate us.

Listen to what Jesus said in John 5:41-44. *"I'm not interested in crowd approval. And do you know why? Because I know you and your crowds. I know that love, especially God's love, is not on your working agenda. I came with the authority of my Father, and you either dismiss me or avoid me. If another came, acting self-important, you would welcome him with open arms. How do you expect to get anywhere with God when you spend all your time jockeying for position with each other, ranking your rivals and ignoring God?"* (MSG)

Paul warns us in Galatians 1:10 not to live to please men, but to please God.

Why do you think you try harder to please people than to please your God? If you don't, what keeps you focused on pleasing God?

The Effects of Self-Righteous Living

There are two very sad outcomes of self-righteous living that keep us blind and in bondage: legalism and criticism. It's amazing to me that these are in direct contrast to what Christ tells us are our two most important commandments.

Instead of *"loving God with all our hearts and souls and minds,"* we become legalistic and turn the most vital relationship possible into a bunch of rules and regulations. When we are caught up in performing, believing we are basically good and trying to please people, we usually become very religious. We focus on our outward behavior and choices, while neglecting our hearts and spirits, which leads to lip service. Our spirituality becomes centered on what we "do" for Christ instead of who we are "becoming" in Christ. Adhering to the rules and the rituals become more important than pursuing the heart of God. My husband says that he was raised in a home where Christianity felt like it was far more about "duty" than it was "desire." Religious homes have the tendency to breed this legalistic pride.

When self-righteous living is dominant, the second most important commandment, *"to love your neighbor as yourself,"* becomes an open door to criticize. When you focus on self-effort, then you are quick to notice when others' attempts fall short. Your eyes turn into microscopes judging others' motives and actions. Your cynicism quenches the Spirit, and this negativity is damaging to others as all people are seeking encouragement, not judgment. This negativity is especially damaging to yourself as you choose blindness to your own sin, focusing only on others'. Your heart is in danger of pushing God's grace away and becoming hardened.

Breaking Free From Pride

The only solution to self-righteous living that our Lord makes perfectly clear throughout Scripture is to kill our pride and embrace humility.

FREEDOM IS WORTH FIGHTING FOR!
"You, my sisters, were called to be free." Galatians 5:13

Never lose sight of the "why" sweet girl. You kill pride and embrace humility because that frees you from the bondage of living out of obligation and sends you to the land of desire and satisfaction.

Note God's view on pride in Psalms 10:4 and Proverbs 16:5,18 and why He would want you to kill it.

Note God's view on humility in 2 Chronicles 7:14 and Philippians 2:3-11 and why he would want you to embrace it.

In what ways does pride need to be put to death in your life?

In what ways does humility need to be put into action in your life?

Mother Teresa - poor and humble

Someone once asked St. Bernard of Clairvaux what the three most important virtues are. He famously replied, "Humility, humility and humility." Humility is a prerequisite for sanctity and, prior to Mother Teresa's death in 1997, people called her a living saint precisely because she lived humility. She wore the same old, patched sandals until they fell apart. Everything she owned fit into a small bag, yet she built one of the largest, most vibrant religious orders of the 20th century.

"Humility is the mother of all virtues; purity, charity and obedience. It is in being humble that our love becomes real, devoted and ardent. If you are humble nothing will touch you, neither praise nor disgrace, because you know what you are." Mother Teresa

Have you embraced humility?

Last Look in the Mirror

 Considering self-righteousness and God's desire for your freedom, ask yourself the following:

What stands out to you about God and His character today?

What is the one thing that you learned about yourself today?

How do these answers relate to your present life? What could they be saying to your mind, emotions, or will?

 With transformation as my goal, what is the one thing I can change/add/stop or continue growing in?

1   "Self-righteousness." *Wikipedia.com*. Wikimedia Foundation, Inc., n.d. Web. 10 Oct. 2013. <http://www.wikpedia.com/dictionary/self-righteous>.
2   "Self-righteous." *Merriam-Webster.com*. Merriam-Webster, n.d. Web. 12 Oct. 2013. <http://www.merriam-webster.com/dictionary/self-righteous>
3   "Holier-than-thou." The American Heritage® Dictionary of the English Language, Fourth Edition. 2003. Houghton Mifflin Company 12 Oct. 2013 <http://www.thefreedictionary.com/holier-than-thou>.

Freedom Is Worth Fighting For

Living in the Land of "What If?": Freedom from the Captivity of Sin

 Lord, quiet my soul right now. Create a space in my heart for just the two of us. Reveal Yourself to me, I pray. Amen.

Make no mistake; I *want* to be a brave woman. I told you that the apostle Paul is my New Testament hero, and he was one brave man of God. I don't know if Paul and fear ever shared the same room; he faced life with courage. I have had some success at bravery as well.

A Time of Bravery

I remember working at a very conservative, private Christian high school where it seemed I had two strikes against me--I was young and I was a woman. I loved the opportunity to challenge young people to make sure their relationship with God wasn't a cultural thing but a very real and personal walk. I longed to see each of them be on fire for God, and I built some amazing relationships with the students.

My relationship with the administration was a different matter. The principal saw me as immature and lacking in my job. It was during a staff meeting one day that I was called on by God to confront my fellow teachers and administration concerning a chapel where we, as leaders, really dropped the ball. We failed to lead our students by our example. This was beyond "scary berries" to me; I was shaking in my boots as I begged God to let someone else say something. Trust me; this was not going to be received well by the people in this room. Finally, I bargained with God and decided that if He really wanted me to do this then He would have the administrator ask if there were any comments or input at the end of our meeting. This had never happened before, so I knew that I was safe.

Oh, yes, you guessed it! First time ever in our meetings, the administrator opens the floor and asks for any additional comments at the end. I am sick to my stomach, my heartbeat is so loud that I am sure everyone around me can hear it, and I can feel the blood rushing to my face. I raise my hand ...I prayed for each word that was about to come out of my mouth...I took a deep breath... and I dove in. I shared what I believe God would have me say, and, like I had feared, it was not well received by my colleagues. However, I knew that I had been faithful to what God asked me to do, and it felt good in the sense that it felt right.

A Time of Cowardice

Let me just get the ball rolling with sharing a few (of my far too many) times I recall wimping out to fear.

I could never see myself putting up with any form of abuse from a guy, but I did. Although I didn't date that much in high school, I did have a few short-lived relationships. I had been seeing this particular boyfriend for a little over a month and the whole way he treated me, talked to me, and looked at me began to change. Good-bye Mr. Charming and hello Mr. Control; but my fear of being rejected and alone kept me from seeing it. So I kept rationalizing his mean comments and name-calling. I thought to myself, "He's just having a rough day," or "He must have a reason for being on edge tonight." Then came the time when his anger turned into pushing me around and poking me hard in the chest. That was when I wimped out. I allowed the fear of him getting even angrier and the fear of him breaking up with me and being without a boyfriend to rule my response: I remained silent. I didn't have the courage to stand up for myself, and I continued the relationship only to have him break-up with me a week later. How sad is that!

I was the first in my family to accept Christ, and I hoped to lead many family members to Him as well. I couldn't imagine passing up an opportunity to witness to my extended family, but I did. My husband and I were vacationing with my extended family on their annual houseboat vacation. Most of us were in the kitchen area hanging out after a heated round of killer Uno, and I was engaged in a casual conversation with various members of my family. Suddenly, one of my cousins piped up from across the room and asked me a point-blank question about my faith. The whole room went dead quiet. Here was my opportunity; I could really take a stand for Jesus--isn't this what I had begged God for when I prayed? And what did I do? Oh yeah, you guessed it--I blew it royally. I freaked out with fear of ridicule, I squandered my open door, and I gave a pat answer that ended the conversation before it ever began. How embarrassing to have to write.

How Brave are You? Take a Look in the Mirror

My two personal favorite definitions for bravery are as follows:
1 - Facing life head on without denial
2 - Not hesitating to do whatever is needed in order to accomplish your mission

According to these two definitions, how brave are you?
1 2 3 4 5 6 7 8 9 10

How brave do you want to be?
1 2 3 4 5 6 7 8 9 10

I believe that for myself and most of you there exists a gap between how brave we are and how brave we want to be. God is deeply concerned about our bravery because He knows it is the pathway to freedom and He always want us to remember that.

FREEDOM IS WORTH FIGHTING FOR!
"You, sisters, were called to be free." Galatians. 5:13

In every facet of life we find fear. It stalks the best of us, and Christians are not immune to it. In order to be brave, we must get rid of our fears.

Fear Takes Us Captive

Where does fear come from according to 2 Timothy 1:7? _____

Every time you feel fear in your life, it's a manifestation of the kingdom of darkness. Fear is bred in the unknown, the "what if's." As women, our minds run rampant to the worst-case scenario and dwell there. In theory, fear is when our mind is "out of control," but in reality, it's when our mind is under the enemy's control.

So, according to 1 John 4:18, what does fear do to us?

Let me add to the list of how Satan uses fear for his purposes in your life:

Fear immobilizes you.
You become so wrapped up in it that you are held back from living life or responding to it.
Fear leads to compromise.
Fear never results in our finest moments; rather it causes us to bargain, concede, and falsely accommodate others.
Fear brings co-dependency and dysfunction to our relationships.
The codependent partner will always struggle with the fear of rejection and the fear of abandonment which prevents her from having a healthy relationship.
Fear causes us to become totally self-centered.
We are consumed with what we are afraid of and how it affects us.
Fear fuels anger, outbursts, and defensiveness.
Fear is unhealthy; it gives us a false sense of protecting our selves.
Fear is behind the need to control.
Fearful thoughts keep chasing each other in a vicious cycle that usually leads downward. Insecurities mount and the loss of control leads to more fear, followed by a paramount desire to maintain the illusion of control.

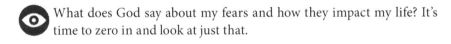 What does God say about my fears and how they impact my life? It's time to zero in and look at just that.

Looking in God's Mirror and Bravely Fighting Fear

As it says in Luke 1:74, we want to be rescued from the hand of our enemies and be able to serve our God without fear. In order to experience this freedom from fear, we must know and believe two things.

1. We Need To Know and Believe God's Command

It is interesting to note that the most frequent biblical command is "Do not fear." God repeats this command, usually in the form of "fear not" or "do not be afraid," even more times than that of our God-given command to love one another. That should tell you something about how badly God wants us to live in Him and not in fear. He is exalted when we live in freedom from fear and each of us chooses to place our trust in the hands of our capable and mighty God.

What do you fear in your life now? What area is hardest to trust Him with?

What do you need to believe in order to lay that fear in His Hands?

2. We Need To Know and Believe God's Character

Isaiah 26:3 instructs us that God will "*keep in perfect peace those whose minds are steadfast because they trust in God.*" Let me remind you who your God is with just looking at a portion of His multi-faceted character.

He is With Us

What name is given to Jesus in Matthew 1:23 and what does it mean?

He is "*with us.*" That word "with" is a giant word when you really understand all that it implies. It means accompanied by or in the same direction as-- therefore, Jesus is accompanying you on His path for your life and He is going in the same direction as you. You are not alone.

God makes a take-to-the-bank promise to each of His children in Hebrews 13:5. What does He promise you as you walk through life together?

But let me share with you what Satan, the father of lies, tells you in your mind...

> *"You should be afraid--you are all alone."*
> *"No one else knows what you are going through or how this*
> *makes you feel."*
> *"You don't think you can do it, do you?"*
> *"What will people think of you?"*

In case you didn't notice, the Enemy wants you to think just about "you." He wants you to dwell on "you." He wants you to completely lose sight of the truth that you are not alone--the God of the Universe is right there with you at every moment. With you. With you. With you.

I have had the opportunity to do several ropes courses, but a few years back was my first opportunity to do a partner high ropes course. Each event of the course was to be done with someone in your group. I will never forget when my dear friend Darlene and I climbed the tall poles to do a very challenging station. At the top of our poles was a set of wires running parallel to each other stretching from our trees to the far trees across the grounds. These were only for our feet. She was to step out onto her wire at the same time I was to step out on mine across from her, and we were to lean towards one another to grab both hands for balance. If you can imagine, the wires and our bodies resulted in a triangular shape.

Now, here was the catch (as if that wasn't enough), as we slowly sidestepped across our wires, the wires themselves began to spread farther apart. The challenge was to try to make it far enough across the wires that Darlene and I would be almost lying flat in the air gripping each other's hands--yeah right!? As we started out across this adventure, a few critical things occurred: we looked each other straight in the eyes and continually communicated, we became completely dependent on one another, and we had white knuckles from our tight grip.

I would give anything for you to be able to feel every aspect of those few moments Darlene and I shared. I was really impacted by the intensity of it, but even more so afterwards. It dawned on me that God had given me the greatest picture of what it means to have Him "with me." He is looking me straight in the eyes, wanting me to communicate with Him constantly, and literally white-knuckling each step of life with me. Dear one, Jesus is white-knuckling it with you too. Whatever you are facing, fear not; you are not alone and your Lord is holding both of your hands tighter than you think.

How does knowing that God is "white-knuckling this life with you" change your perspective?

He is Good

When I was in the Philippines, every church service I attended I heard the pastor say to the congregation, "Jesus is good" and the people would respond, "All the time!" Then the pastor said, "And all the time," and the body shouted, "Jesus is good!" Interesting isn't it that they didn't say, "Some of the time Jesus is good," "Most of the time Jesus is good," or "He sure is good when my life is going good?" I believe my Philippine brothers and sisters, who live in third world conditions, have already settled a truth in their hearts--God does all things well; He is good all the time.

When we are fearful, we have lost sight of God's goodness. God's goodness has to do with the perfections of His person and the kindness of His acts. Both ideas occur together in one verse in the Psalms: "You are good and do good" (Psalms 119:68). We might trust God as long as our fear doesn't come to fruition, but when we play out the "worst case scenarios" in our minds then we lose any belief that His sovereignty is for His Glory and for our good.

What will help you trust in God's goodness from Psalms 34:8 and 100:5?

Because God is Himself the highest and greatest good, He is also the source and fountain of all other good. He does good things. He extends His goodness to others. It is His nature to be kind, generous, and benevolent, to demonstrate good will toward men, and to take great pleasure in making them happy. Every good thing we now enjoy or ever hope to enjoy flows from Him, and no good thing has ever existed or ever will exist that does not come from His good hand.

How is God good in your life right now? How does God's goodness affect your fear?

His Love is Perfect

Do you know that God promises in Psalms138:8 that "*He will accomplish what concerns you*"? (NASB) He is not distant or busy or looking the other way. Even though He sits on the Throne of All, He declares that He will perfect and hone and shape what He began in you the moment you became His, and He will continue to do this until the day of Christ's return (Philippians 1:6).

Beloved, the love He loves you with is a perfect love. Literally, this unconditional, sacrificial love does what for you according to 1 John 4:16-18?

A dear friend always challenged me when I was fearful with the same question, "Christie, what is the very worst thing you can imagine happening?" In other words, what are you most afraid of in this situation or relationship? Playing the worst case scenario game might seem like a doomsday approach to battling fear, but her point was to get me to view the most unimaginable scene in light of Who God is. In the end, His perfect love always trumps the fear.

Let me illustrate this with my own fear of becoming an early widow.

> *Worst Case Scenario*: My husband dies tomorrow.

> *God's Character*: He loves me and promises to be my husband.
>> He will provide for my financial situation out of His faithfulness.
>> He will be the Father to my fatherless children.
>> He will supply me with grace that will sufficiently meet my every need.

> *Possibilities For How God Could Use This For His Glory*:
>> What if that is exactly what one of our kids needed to follow Christ whole-heartedly?
>> What if I am called to minister to young widows and begin a new ministry?
>> What if that is what one of Mark's employees needed to reflect on his life and finally put his family first?

This exercise is not meant to have us fixate on a million "what ifs" which will, most likely, never even occur. It is meant to have you and I focus on the character of our God and not our fear!

Now, it's your turn. Choose one of your fears.
Fear:
Worst Case Scenario:
God's Character:

Possibilities For How God Could Use This For His Glory:

Doesn't the perfect love of Jesus cause your fear to subside when you turn your focus off of you and onto the character of our Mighty God?

Precious one, the way to battle your fear is not to hover around the worst case scenario, but to literally take your Jesus smack dab into the middle of that possible scenario and believe Who He is. He and His love cast out your fears.

Last Look in the Mirror

Considering fear and God's desire for your freedom, ask yourself the following:

What stands out to you about God and His character today?

What is the one thing that you learned about yourself today?

How do these answers relate to your present life? What could they be saying to your mind, emotions, or will?

With transformation as my goal, what is the one thing I can change/ add/stop or continue growing in?

Freedom Is Worth Fighting For

My Worries

Living in the Land of Anxiety: Freedom from the Captivity of Sin

How is it possible to clear your mind from everything occupying it right now? Naturally, it's not. So, how about supernaturally? Ask the Holy Spirit to clear your mind and enable you to focus on what He wants to teach you today.

Peeking in the Mirror at How Women Worry

As young women we worry about our weight, family, clothing choices, our appearance, safety, our future, our grades, our dating life, sex, our boyfriends or lack of one, our body, hormones, peer pressure, our friends or lack of them, getting a job, where to go to college, not having enough money, what to do after college graduation, marriage, not being successful, and the list goes on. We are masters at worrying. Sadly, the older we grow, the better we get at it and the more things we add to our life to worry about. Let's face it, when you think of a worry wart, you don't picture a guy, do you? You picture a girl. And it's not surprising when you consider the facts:

- "2.6 million women suffer from generalized anxiety disorder alone, and worry is a key part of this.
- Women are twice as a likely as men to develop an anxiety disorder. One study tracked anxiety in children and found that by the time girls reached adolescence they had six times the rate of generalized anxiety disorder than boys.
- Anxiety disorders are the number one mental health problem among women, according to the National Institutes of Mental Health." [1]

Research shows that women tend to perceive more risk in situations than men do, worry more about financial security than men do, worry more about health concerns than men do, to name a few.

Not only do we worry more, but I believe we worry in more detail about what we are worrying about. Studies show that we, as women, have less mastery over the skills needed to deal with stress. Coupled with our high component towards nurture and relationship, we are easily lead to dwell in the land of anxiety. And once we are in that land, we explore it fully! We walk down every road of opinion, hike every trail of possibility, swim in every lake of "what if," climb every tree of possible ramification, dig into every tunnel of potential threat, and cross every divide of concern. Or should I say, that I know I have, and that I know I do.

What are you worrying about now? Or what is the last thing you worried about?

What Does Worry Do to Us?

Take a moment to really think about these outcomes:
- Worry exhausts us. It physically wears us out and can even make us sick.
- Worry interferes with appetite, sleep, and job performance.
- Worry can cause high anxiety and even lead to panic attacks.
- Worry steals our peace because it is the opposite of faith.
- Worry torments us by pulling us in different directions.
- Worry keeps us from reality since 90% of what we worry about never comes to pass.

- Worry raises cortisol levels in your body (secreted by your adrenal glands) which promotes weight gain, especially in the abdomen area.
- Worry can lead to harmful lifestyle habits or addictions--overeating, cigarette smoking, alcohol, drugs.

It is time to get to the root of our worries. We don't need wrinkles before our time! There is only one place to ever go for the truth that we are looking for.

You Can't Be Free If You're Worrying – Get Rid of Worry

Worry keeps you from experiencing freedom and living the abundant life that Jesus called you to. It may begin with a small, just-for-a-second worry that feels like running into a cobweb, but it will turn into thick, heavy twisted ropes completely entangling you, tripping you up, and sometimes even choking you. You need to be diligent about fighting worry in your life.

Paul wrote a passage in Philippians that gives us complete instructions for how to combat this self-induced anxiety that imprisons us. So, let's dig into it.

Read Philippians 4:4-7 three times: once silently, once out loud, and once dramatically.

FIRST STEP

To begin with, Paul reminds us to **rejoice**. When there is something we are concerned about, rejoicing is about the last thing we feel like doing. Complaining, listing possible problems, and pitying ourselves seem far more fitting, but that's not what we are instructed to do.

Why do you think rejoicing is the best place to start in getting rid of worry?

There is a profound difference between rejoicing and being happy. God is not telling us, "Don't worry. Be happy."

How would you explain the difference between joy and happiness?

To rejoice is to choose a constant, inward delight that is independent of life's circumstances or people's choices. It is knowledge deep within that enables you to trust the heart of God when you don't understand the hand of God, the pain you are forced to deal with, or the chaos of life. It is a huge, perplexing witness of the Supernatural living within you to others.

So, how do you rejoice? You go back to your cornerstone--Jesus Christ. He never changes, cracks, or needs repair. He is your rock and your firm foundation. If you belong to Jesus, what are some of the foundational truths from Scripture you can embrace?

- He is sitting on His sovereign throne never getting up to take a break or walk away.
- You are His daughter and your name has been written in the Book of Life.
- His love for you is sealed. Nothing in heaven or earth has the ability to separate you from His love.
- God's plans cannot be thwarted and He has a plan for your life.
- You have been given the Holy Spirit to empower you to each and every thing you have been called to do for Him.

These are a mere sampling, but each one is worth a lifetime of rejoicing over. On a scale of 1-10, how well do you choose rejoice over worry? _____

Make your own Top 10 Truths to Rejoice Over list. I encourage you to copy this onto your own paper as well and keep it somewhere you can read through when needed.

SECOND STEP

Next, Paul reminds us to **relax**. Why? I know he says it to me because when I am worrying, I am anything but relaxed. I am agitated, my voice can escalate, my shoulders and neck are tense, and my stomach can be nauseous.

Yet, we are told to relax in these verses because the Lord is near. He's not distant; He's at hand. Worry says, "Where is God?" To relax is to remind yourself that God says, "I am right here by your side. You are not forgotten."

What does it mean to you that your God is right by your side 24 hours a day, 7 days a week?

Can God forget about you? Psalms 139:17-18

The Lord is also near in the sense of His second coming--His return to come take His Bride home. How does that particular truth give you perspective and cause your worry to cease?

On a scale of 1-10, how well do you relax instead of worry? _____

THIRD STEP

Lastly, Paul reminds you to **rest in prayer**. When you are worried and feeling pulled in different directions, where do you turn first? Do you turn to your strangling thoughts, to your friends, to your family, to the internet, to Dr. Phil or Oprah...where do you go? God's Word makes it clear that we should go to God if we want freedom and peace.

"Do not be anxious about anything, but in every situation, by prayer and petition, with thanksgiving, present your requests to God." Philippians 4:6

Freedom comes from taking that wasted energy being used on apprehension and putting it to good use. Carry your anxiety to your Father!

I find it very interesting that God doesn't just say we should pray about it, but He gives us three components of prayer that are critical for us to implement. The word "prayer" in this verse carries the idea of adoration, devotion, and worship. What can you learn about adoration from Matthew 6:9 and Psalms 51:15?

How does declaring the majesty and greatness of our God bring us rest?

It's far too easy to hurry past our praises to God and His character. I know that I often find myself tearing open the doors, rushing into His throne room, and spouting off my "give me" or "do this please" or "change this" lists versus meditating on who my God is first.

The word "supplication" indicates an earnest sharing of one's needs and problems. This is not a half-hearted cry but an invitation to pour out our hearts with very specific requests. There is a sense of desperation and spiritual intensity.

How do you see this authentic energy in 1 Kings 8:28 and Matthew 7:7-8?

Consider what you are worrying about presently in your life. What specific requests do you need to make known to your Father?

Once your heart has been laid bare before Him with anything and everything you are seeking, then God directs us to pray with thanksgiving.

The word "thankfulness" is connected with our prayer and gives context for our entire frame of mind. We come to God recognizing all that we have to be thankful for up to this point and move forward in faith, knowing that we will be thankful for the way God uses this circumstance in our life as well. Thanksgiving is the surest mark of a soul free from care and of a heart surrendered to His sovereign will.

What do Psalms 9:1 and 50:23 say to you about thanksgiving?

On a scale 1-10, how well do you rest in prayer versus worry? _____

Test these truths out for yourselves.
Rejoice over God
Relax because your Lord is near
Rest in prayer that worships, seeks, and thanks.

Listen to what will happen as a result.
"Don't fret or worry. Instead of worrying, pray. Let petitions and praises shape your worries into prayers, letting God know your concerns. Before you know it, a sense of God's wholeness, everything coming together for good, will come and settle you down. It's wonderful what happens when Christ displaces worry at the center of your life." Philippians 4:6-7 (MSG)

Who wouldn't want Christ Himself to displace the worry at the center of your life? Wow!

A Look in Paul's Mirror

The Example of Paul

So many things to worry about, yet Paul didn't because he wrote what to do and he chose to actually do those things--time, after time, after time. Do you realize that Paul had more opportunities than most of us ever will to be a consummate worrier? As he wrote the words in Philippians, he was under house arrest with a guard chained to him in Rome. His heart had been aching to preach the gospel to Rome for a very long time and the Spirit finally lead him there, yet Paul ends up imprisoned. His case is about to come up, and he knows very well that he could be beheaded.

But this wasn't his first round at facing extremely difficult situations. You see, he was chased out of towns, had people attempt to stone him, was beaten many times, was hated by many and mistrusted by most, had been shipwrecked several times, in and out of prisons, flogged too many times to count, spent a day and night in the sea, received 39 lashes from the Jews multiple times, and went hungry, cold, and sleepless. How could he not spend most of his energy worrying?

The answer lies in this verse: *"For me to live is Christ, and to die is gain"* (Philippians 1:21). You see, Paul had already given his life away. Therefore, while he still had breath on earth, he knew how to rejoice, relax, and rest in prayer.

The question, sweet sister, is do you?

Last Look in the Mirror

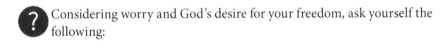 Considering worry and God's desire for your freedom, ask yourself the following:

What stands out to you about God and His character today?

What is the one thing that you learned about yourself today?

How do these answers relate to your present life? What could they be saying to your mind, emotions, or will?

 With transformation as my goal, what is the one thing I can change/add/stop or continue growing in?

I wish I could walk into the room right now, wherever you are doing this study, and just give you a giant hug. This is a hard week and you have done so well. Hang in there--only one more day of study and you will have reached the halfway mark!

[1]   Hazlett-Stevens, Holly. *Women Who Worry Too Much*. Oakland, CA: New Harbinger Publications, 2005.

Freedom Is Worth Fighting For

My Strongholds: Part One

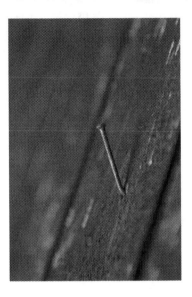

Living in the Land of Bondage: Freedom from the Captivity of Sin

✋ I am bringing you before God today and asking for Him to anoint wherever you are sitting as holy ground. I am asking Him to send one of His angels to stand guard for you as you seek to discover whether Satan has taken any ground in your heart. Please ask God to do the same.

A Parable Makes the Point

An old parable thought to be told by a Haitian pastor makes the point:

A certain man wanted to sell his house for two thousand dollars. Another man wanted to buy it very badly, but he was a poor man and didn't have the full price. After much bargaining, the owner agreed to sell the house to the man for a thousand dollars, but the reduced price came with a stipulation. The owner would sell the house, but he would keep ownership of a large nail protruding from over the front door.

Several years later, the original owner decided he wanted to buy the house back. Understandably, the new owner was unwilling to sell. As a result, the original owner went out, found the carcass of a dead dog in the street, and hung it from the nail he still owned. Soon the house became unlivable, and the family was forced to sell to the owner of the nail.

The Haitian pastor concluded the story, *"If we leave the devil with even one small peg in our life, he will return to hang his rotting garbage on it."*

Each nail in the wall of our house represents a stronghold--a lie we have bought into. According to Neil T. Anderson, author of *Victory Over Darkness,* these nails are "driven into the walls of our minds either through repetition over time or through one-time traumatic experiences."[1] If we don't intentionally put effort into removing the nails, then Satan begins to hang carcasses on each one, causing us to live with the constant stench of rotting death in our lives. The stench only grows worse as time goes on; to the point we actually become accustomed to it, no longer smelling anything foul. While we may not smell the carcasses anymore, we can still see them. And out of the fear others might see them too, we futilely try to hide them by covering them up or just acting like they don't exist. Consequentially, we become enslaved to these death nails and our entire lives revolve around them in some way. Feeling hopeless, our freedom is lost and our intimacy with God will be taken from us as we bow to the enemy who owns each of our nails.

Christian Armor Ministries says that "We can be genuinely born-again, and sincere in our faith, but chronically struggle with thoughts, emotions, and habits that wage war against our relationship with Christ. We pray, we study, and we attempt to discipline ourselves, but often find our 'problem' is resistant to real change." [2] In areas where the strongholds are established, that nails are driven in, an individual is either unable to consistently follow God's word or is unable to accept it because these spiritual strongholds have an excessive influence on him.

Looking at Myself in the Mirror

Younger sister, I am sad to say that I have so many holes in the walls of my life from the enemy's nails. I understand buying into lies. I understand being deceived. I understand nails. I understand rationalizing what I am involved in. I understand the smell of dead, rotting meat. I understand the feelings of being overwhelmed and defeated far too quickly. I understand making sure no one else finds out what I am thinking. BUT, I also understand what freedom feels like and there is no greater feeling!

Freedom is worth fighting for!

Since I am going to ask you to come face to face with your strongholds, your nails, I want you to know that I will lead the way in sharing. As we progress through this lesson, I am not asking you to do anything that I haven't done already myself.

Looking in God's Mirror

God wants you to clearly understand His Word and stand firm upon it, grasping your sword of truth at all times.

Let's delve into the central verses about strongholds in the New Testament.

"For though we live in the world, we do not wage war as the world does. The weapons we fight with are not the weapons of the world. On the contrary, they have divine power to demolish strongholds. We demolish arguments and every pretension that sets itself up against the knowledge of God, and we take captive every thought to make it obedient to Christ." 2 Corinthians 10:3-5

What kind of battle is a stronghold? _____ of the Flesh _____ of the Spirit
What kind of weapons are we given to fight with? _____
Where do these strongholds exist? _____ Mind _____ Body _____ Soul
What are these strongholds specifically against?

What is our goal that will bring freedom?

"Don't you know that when you offer yourselves to someone as obedient slaves (allow a nail to be driven), you are slaves of the one you obey?" Romans 6:16

Each stronghold causes you to be enslaved to whom?

What does it mean to be a slave?

What do you think the goal might be of the "master", the one who now has the power?

Spiritual strongholds are those whispering lies of Satan that have grown into a place of captivity. We left a vulnerable opening, and Satan took full advantage. Now is the time to recapture yourself and your freedom. Now is the time to take each and every nail out of your walls. Let's do this.

How Do We Bravely Break Free From A Stronghold?

Look Back * Look Within * Look Up * Look
Through a New Mind * Look Out

LOOK BACK

You need to **look back** into your history at three different areas to discover possible present strongholds--you need to look at your family, you need to look at your hurts, and you need to look at your sin.

Look Back at Your Family

We can't break free from a stronghold we don't even know exists. So our first step is to take inventory of our life and see if any nails have been hammered in without our knowing it. Let me go first...

As I looked back at my family history, I noticed three sins that my family kept being drawn to: adultery, pornography, and alcohol/drug addiction. So, I asked myself, "Do I struggle with any of these as a stronghold?" I don't now, but I did struggle with pornography as a teenager. Since I am still vulnerable to these areas, I asked myself what protection do I have in place to guard my heart so the enemy can't get a nail hammered into my wall?

I want you to fill in the following chart about your family and how each member has affected you positively and/or negatively towards your own freedom and living out God's truth. In other words, in what ways have their lives modeled or encouraged you to go deeper in your walk with Jesus or what lies/nails have you witnessed in their lives that could hinder your following of Christ? (Deuteronomy 5:9)

If you didn't know some or all of these family members, then substitute them with the caregivers that you have known.

MATERNAL SIDE	PATERNAL SIDE
Grandpa - positive	Grandpa - positive
Grandpa - negative	Grandpa - negative
Grandma - positive	Grandma - positive
Grandma - negative	Grandma - negative
Mother - positive	Father - positive
Mother - negative	Father - negative

Do you see any repeated patterns in your family--positive or negative?

Do you see any generational sin--one that has been passed down from your grandparents to your parents or from your parents to you or your sibling(s)?

NOTE - This is not about casting blame or pointing fingers. This is about removing the carcasses and nails that have been passed along. In fact, can you perhaps see any reasons why your family has struggled with some of their issues?

What have been the 2 biggest positive influences from your family?

What have been the 2 strongest negative influences from your family?

Look Back at Your Hurts

As I reflected upon my hurts from the past, I knew that I had been left with scars from the nails that were unwillingly hammered into the walls of my heart. My unstable and inconsistent family life left me with deep trust issues, the lie that I had to perform to be loved, the deception that perfection was the norm, deep insecurity and feelings of worthlessness, and a hyper self-conscientiousness.

I would like you to make a list of how you have been deeply hurt by other people and their sin. These instances were not your choices, but you have been left with the scars. Include anyone you have not forgiven or are still angry at.

Look Back at Your Sin

Lastly, I asked myself what was the sin that I couldn't seem to shake or get victory over? That was simple--my thought life and the lies that it wouldn't affect anybody else and that it wasn't a big deal since I wasn't going to act on it.

Record any repetitive sin that you feel bound by. This is the sin that you have asked forgiveness for a million times. Nobody else may know about this one, but you do. You know exactly which sin or sins. (Jeremiah 17:9, Hebrews 12:1-2)

As we look back, recognize that we can be blind to our history and how it has affected us. If we've spent our whole life with these particular habits, perspectives, hurts, behaviors, or thoughts then we are quite comfortable with them. We might even think that they are just "who we are" rather than how we are imprisoned. Take a moment to bow and ask the Holy Spirit to help reveal any blind spots to your present day strongholds.

Now it's your turn to take inventory. Between all three exercises, make a list here of what God has shown you as possible strongholds in your life today, resulting from your family, your hurt, or your sin.

LOOK WITHIN

Now it is time to *look within* in order to clean house in our hearts. It is time for confession--the opposite of denial or concealment. Confession is owning up to something you know or believe, and telling it forthrightly to all who should hear it. I want to give you the opportunity for cleansing by walking you through your family's past, your hurt, and your sin.

"Blessed is the one who perseveres under trial because, having stood the test, that person will receive the crown of life that the Lord has promised to those who love him. When tempted, no one should say, "God is tempting me." For God cannot be tempted by evil, nor does he tempt anyone; but each person is tempted when they are dragged away by their own evil desire and enticed." James 1:12-14

"Above all else, guard your heart, for everything you do flows from it." Prov. 4:23

Confession: Your Family's Past

It is wise to recognize generational sin and understand the specific sins that you are vulnerable to. It is wise to put on the full armor of God with prayer, memorization of Scripture, and preventative plans.

Confess any of your struggles with sin that are similar to those your family has dealt with or is currently dealing with. List struggles here.

Ask God to protect your heart in those areas.

Choose a verse to memorize according to each struggle listed above. Use the concordance in your Bible or search online for verses that deal with your particular sin.

Devise a plan of protection--what will you do if confronted with the temptation? (List applicable verses and your plan of protection on a separate piece of paper.) This is well worth the extra effort.

Confession: Your Hurt

You don't confess sin that has been done against you, but you do need to confess any unforgiveness or bitterness you have allowed to take root as a direct result of the pain. Remember that granting forgiveness does not condone or erase what has been done to you in any way. It is an act of obedience that offers you the opportunity to reveal the beauty of Jesus Christ and, as you do, be given your own ticket to healing and freedom. (Be advised, in circumstances of abuse, molestation, or rape, please seek professional counseling.)

> *"Bear with each other and forgive one another if any of you has a grievance against someone. Forgive as the Lord forgave you."* Colossians 3:13

> *"See to it that no one falls short of the grace of God and that no bitter root grows up to cause trouble and defile many."* Hebrews 12:15

Take time to acknowledge your hurt by writing how the wrongs done to you made you feel. You need to recognize that you have a right to your feelings.

Confess any bitterness or withholding forgiveness that you don't have a right to.

Confession: Your Sin

Today is the day you can release yourself from the bondage of habitual sin that is controlling you. Aren't you sick and tired of the maggots and death it brings?

Name your sin that has you in its grip. Write it on a piece of paper.

> *"If we confess our sins, he is faithful and just and will forgive us our sins and purify us from all unrighteousness."* 1 John 1:9

According to the *International Standard Bible Encyclopedia*, the radical meaning of confession is "acknowledgment," or "avowal" with the implication of a change of conviction or of course of conduct on the part of the subject. [3] You don't confess with the goal of being forgiven. You confess with the goal of repentance--making a turnaround in your behavior, not wanting to continue with that sin in the future. Trust me, God is waiting to purify you and free you and gather you close.

> *"Have mercy on me, O God, according to your unfailing love;*
> *according to your great compassion blot out my transgressions. Wash*
> *away all my iniquity and cleanse me from my sin. For I know my*
> *transgressions, and my sin is always before me. Against you, you*
> *only, have I sinned and done what is evil in your sight; so you are*
> *right in your verdict and justified when you judge." Ps. 51:1-4*

Confess--acknowledge--come to agreement with God that this sin is directly against Him. Acknowledge that you will never overcome it on your own. Rip that piece of paper with the sin written on it into many little pieces and throw it away in a garbage can. Bless Him and praise Him for cleansing you completely.

> *"For sin shall no longer be your master..." Rom. 6:14*

Ask yourself what lie you have bought into that entices you with this sin. Now write on a piece of paper a Bible verse that states the truth about this issue.

Memorize this verse and believe that only Jesus can meet the desires of your heart and the longings of your soul.

Thank Jesus Christ for paying the price so that sin has no power over you--so that (name your particular sin) has no rule over you.

Next week we will continue with the part two of Bravely Breaking Free from Your Stronghold. We will cover the last three parts:

Look Up ~ Look Through a New Mind ~ Look Out.

Last Look in the Mirror

Considering strongholds and God's desire for your freedom, ask yourself the following:

What stands out to you about God and His character today?

What is the one thing that you learned about yourself today?

How do these answers relate to your present life? What could they be saying to your mind, emotions, or will?

 With transformation as my goal, what is the one thing I can change/add/stop or continue growing in?

1   Anderson, Neil T. *Victory Over Darkness*. Ventura, CA: Regal Books, 1990. Print.

2   "Spiritual Strongholds." *Christian Armor Ministries*. The Grace Net, n.d. Web. 19 Mar. 2012. <christianarmor.net>.

3   Bromiley, William. "Confess." Vol. 3. University of Michigan: W.B. Eerdmans, 1986. N. pag. Print

WRAP UP TO YOUR THIRD WEEK OF STUDY

Freedom is worth fighting for...may that become your mantra. You have spent the past five days looking at many of the ways Satan tries to enslave us: through your emotional baggage that hasn't been unpacked, through your legalism that has blinded you, through your fears that immobilize you, through your worry that has accomplished nothing, and through your strongholds where Satan has spied a vulnerability and literally made you his captive. God cries out to you that He has never desired you to live this way, and this week He has asked you to look in the mirror and determine to make a move! Fellow fighter, put your boxing gloves on. Get out your sharpest sword. Throw on your helmet and pads. It's time to do battle!

In the upcoming days you will finish learning about breaking spiritual strongholds, the two critical elements that freedom requires, and a glimpse of two gifts that freedom leads to. Be excited.

As You Start Your Fourth Week of Study

If I told you that tennis was the best racquet sport around for you to play and I wanted you to go try it, but I didn't equip you with a tennis racquet and ball, it would be foolish. In the same way, I can't champion the land of freedom, yet not equip you with the essential items needed to get you there. Trust me, I have tried repairing clothing items with hot glue or duct tape or safety pins, and failed miserably because I didn't have what was actually needed--a needle and thread!

You won't find freedom on your own. God teaches us that we must have His Holy Spirit and His Truth. So don't be silly and try to find freedom any other way. Once you've discovered true freedom, you will be thrilled with the amazing places that freedom takes you!

Come with a fresh desire to learn from God's Word this week as He equips you for your journey to freedom.

FREEDOM IS WORTH FIGHTING FOR

DAY 16: My Strongholds (part two)
How can you break free from the heavy chains that enslave you?

DAY 17: His Spirit
How much control does the Holy Spirit have of your life?

DAY 18: His Truth
Is His truth transforming your mind, your heart, and your life the way He has intended it to?

DAY 19: Freed to Love
Is your freedom leading you to love? To love more? To love differently?

DAY 20: Freed to Bear Fruit
How much fruit are you bearing as a result of your freedom in Jesus Christ?

Freedom Is Worth Fighting For

My Strongholds: Part Two

Living in the Land of Bondage: Freedom from the Captivity of Sin

✋ Selah. Pause and ask God again to protect this time together in His Word, as you explore ways Satan has driven in one of his lying, filthy nails. Ask His Spirit to go before you and make His path to freedom real and clear.

Remember the Parable with a Powerful Point

The Haitian pastor concluded the story, *"If we leave the devil with even one small peg in our life, he will return to hang his rotting garbage on it."*

Remember that each nail in the wall of your house represents a stronghold--a lie we have bought into. These nails were driven in throughout your childhood and past, only to invite Satan to come and hang his rotting garbage on them. Beth Moore defines a stronghold as anything that you start holding onto that ends up holding onto you. So our job is to believe freedom is worth fighting for and rid ourselves of each and every nail! We will even talk about how to fill the holes we are left with.

Looking in God's Mirror

We have so much incredible truth to cover today that we are not going to waste any time, but just dive right back in where we left off. Re-read our key verse:

"For though we live in the world, we do not wage war as the world does. The weapons we fight with are not the weapons of the world. On the contrary, they have divine power to demolish strongholds. We demolish arguments and every pretension that sets itself up against the knowledge of God, and we take captive every thought to make it obedient to Christ." 2 Corinthians 10:3-5

How Do We Bravely Break Free From a Stronghold?

Look Back * Look Within * Look Up * Look
Through a New Mind * Look Out

You spent time on Day 15 **looking back** at your family's history of sin, past hurts that were committed against you, and your past sins. You compiled a list of possible strongholds.

Then you took the time to **look within** and agree with God over which of these were actually strongholds, which sins you needed to confess, and whether you were still withholding forgiveness that needed to be extended.

After looking back and looking within, you should be able to state what nails you want to be free from. I told you that I would go first--pornography didn't have a stronghold in my life but I did need a plan to protect myself from it. So I chose my verses and who I would keep myself accountable to. Alcohol/drug addictions didn't leave a nail in my wall because I chose a "zero tolerance" policy, and adultery didn't get a peg in me either because I had lived as a child of divorce and was fully committed to never having a back door out of my marriage. However, my nails were insecurity, perfectionism, my thought life, and not willing to trust others. By walking through the first two places to look, it's like we have raised the hammer's claw to remove each nail, but we still have more places to look on our journey to living Nail-Free!

LOOK UP

Now with awareness of your strongholds, a cleansed heart and a bent knee, it is time to **look up** at the One who sits on His throne, for this is where your help comes from. God doesn't just have rule over the universe and the stars, He has rule over you and me.

We need to look outside of ourselves and see that God has a right to rule in our lives. How can we claim Him as our Master, yet we live our own life according to our own rules? We can't have it both ways. The sooner we understand that only He can reveal our strongholds, only He can pull out the nails, and only He can bring the victory, the sooner we will surrender in obedience to our God. He will give us the truth needed to break the chains of the bondage we are held captive by, but we have to listen to Him because it only works His way.

Look up 2 Chronicles 20:15 and Romans 8:9-14 and glean what you can about who is fighting the battle and how it is to be led.

Seriously, after reading these verses, you may think that you have nothing to do or no part in this journey to freedom. But that isn't correct either. We need to acknowledge, confess, and surrender.

Remind yourself what God teaches you about surrender in Psalms 9:10 and Romans 12:1.

Once you've declared your dependence on the Almighty, how do you present yourself to Him according to Romans 6:11-23?

I learned the hard way. I strived and I strived to break my habitual sin. I worked so hard to fight against the lies I had bought into. I battled and strained and kept trying more things, and guess what I found out? The harder I tried to resist, the more my strongholds persisted! What we resist persists, but what we surrender God takes care of. Can't you picture it? What I am striving to fight in my own strength has my puny hands all over it. Yet what I lay at Christ's feet in surrender, He can now grab ahold of with His perfect all-powerful Hands. It may sound like a very subtle difference, but it isn't at all. Trust me, it's huge.

When I would hear my self-talk of "You know you are worthless…Nobody wants to be close to you…Why can't you get it through your head Christie? You aren't loved," I kept trying to argue with my thoughts and telling myself to stop thinking them. You know what happens when you tell yourself to stop thinking thoughts for pity's sake; it's all you can think about! I needed to keep throwing myself at the feet of Jesus declaring over and over, "I need You. I am desperate for You. I cannot do this. Please intervene."

We don't necessarily need more discipline, we need more dependence.

LOOK THROUGH A NEW MIND

As you've looked back to become aware, looked within to confess and acknowledge, and looked up to the only source of freedom, now the time has come to **look through a new mind.** You literally need to reprogram the way you think.

My husband Mark only drives trucks--big crew cab, slightly lifted trucks. (You should see the comedy show on Sundays as I try climbing in and out of these trucks in any kind of a straight skirt.) Anyways, his newest truck is a diesel, and he has hammered into my head that I can only put diesel fuel into the gas tank because that truck will only run on diesel fuel. I can hear him now, "Christie, make sure you only go to gas stations with green handles on the pumps and only use those "green handle" pumps for my truck!"

My husband had driven to Canada to do some concrete work for a family friend's daughter and husband as a gift. They were newly married and didn't have much money and he knew this would bless them. (Not to mention, my husband is the most giving man I know.) The morning he was going to return home, he only made it a few miles when his engine started acting really weird, smoking and sputtering. Something was wrong. His truck just wasn't running right. He pulled over to the side of the road and noticed that his gas tank had been filled up, but he hadn't done that. He grabbed his cell and called his buddy to ask him if he knew anything about this. Sure enough, our family friend had wanted to express his thanks to Mark for being so generous with his kids that he had taken Mark's truck to fill it with gas--only he filled it with regular unleaded gasoline! Yes, it was a disaster! The truck's fuel tank had to be completely drained, the entire system cleaned, and then re-fueled with diesel gasoline. It was a very expensive gasoline mistake.

Dear one, we, too, are meant to drive our minds on only one kind of fuel--the truth. Every time you try to put another kind of fuel into it--the lies--I promise you, you will smoke and sputter and break down. When you recognize you are operating on lies, you need to do the same thing Mark's mechanic did: you need to drain, clean, empty, and get rid of every lie. And no engine will run on no fuel, so there is no such thing as leaving a tank or your mind empty. It needs to be filled--filled with the truth.

"For though we live in the world, we do not wage war as the world does. The weapons we fight with are not the weapons of the world. On the contrary, they have divine power to demolish strongholds. We demolish arguments and every pretension that sets itself up against the knowledge of God, and we take captive every thought to make it obedient to Christ." 2 Corinthians10:3-5

Emptying Your Mind of the Wrong Fuel: The Lies

Where do you think these arguments, pretensions (claims), and thoughts come from and what can you learn about this strategy? John 8:44, 2 Corinthians 11:3

Each time you expose a lie, you defeat Satan. Sister, he has no power over you because, as 1 John 4:4 tells us that *"the one who is in you is greater than the one who is in the world."* Therefore, the only power the enemy has in your life is the power you give him. You give the enemy fuel each time you accept his lies into your mind and/or act on them.

Here are some of the lies that I had bought into:
"I need to earn love."
"If it's not perfect, then I have failed."
"I have no worth or value on my own."
"Everybody is critiquing me."
"No one can be trusted. It's only a matter of time."

Take your list of strongholds and recall what is the lie or lies you have bought into with each one. Expose these lies by writing each lie down.

Empty your tanks of this destructive fuel! Ask God to help you immediately recognize deception in the future. We can learn the most effective way to recognize deception from our US Treasury. Those who become counterfeit experts do not waste their time looking at counterfeit currency. Instead, they spend all their time studying true currency, so that an officer can instantly detect anything that is off with a counterfeit bill.

In the same way, once we have emptied our minds of the deceptions and lies, it is time to fill it with the truth and only the truth, so that we can identify and expose future falsehoods for what they truly are.

Filling Your Mind with the Right Fuel: The Truth

I recall a time when my daughter, Taylor, was struggling with this very thing and I was trying to help her learn this most important life lesson. I told her that her favorite teddy bear was now called "Teddy the Truth Bear" and when she would start talking about any lie she was buying into out loud, I would redirect her to Teddy. "But what does Teddy the Truth say?" When she felt like it was easier to embrace the lie, I told her to take Teddy to bed with her and hold on tight to him! One of the most important lessons we need to learn in our entire lives is that every facet of our life needs to be based on truth. Truth is what lights our way and guides us. Truth is what never changes. Truth is our anchor for every storm. Truth is what revives the cold and hard places of our heart. Truth is what inspires us to go forward and be more like Jesus. Truth is what gives us hope. Truth is what keeps us from straying. Truth is what gives us our security. Truth is what unites our community of Christ-followers. Truth is what breaks every chain and sets us free! And our gracious and merciful God has given us His precious and powerful truth--Genesis through Revelation. We are blessed indeed.

There might be a fuel shortage in the United Sates and we might have to pay high gas prices, but when it comes to the fuel of God's truth, we have it in abundance. The question lies in whether or not we are filling our minds with His Truth.

Glean wisdom from Romans 12:2 and Ephesians 6:10-14. What do they say to you?

The time has come to fill your mind with truth. Take your list of lies and now find a verse of truth to battle each lie with. You can use my list as an example…

- I need to earn love. *"While we were still sinners, Christ died for us."* Romans 5:8
- If it's not perfect, then I have failed. *"Whatever you do, work at it with all your heart, as working for the Lord, not human masters,"* Colossians 3:23

- I have no worth or value on my own. *"I praise you because I am fearfully and wonderfully made; your works are wonderful, I know that full well."* Psalms 139: 14
- Everybody is critiquing me. *"Am I now trying to win the approval of human beings, or of God? Or am I trying to please people? If I were still trying to please people, I would not be a servant of Christ."* Galatians 1:10
- No one can be trusted. It's only a matter of time. *"It is better to take refuge in the Lord, than to trust in humans."* Psalms 118:8

When breaking free from a stronghold or resisting the temptation to buy into a lie, there is no better idea than to have truth verses written on cards to keep in your purse, car, at your desk, or by your mirror. Your weapon is your sword-- keep it handy and close. It doesn't do you any good somewhere you can't find it. I recently bought my daughter 3x5 cards on a spiral holder so she could do just that.

LOOK OUT

You are now free in Christ if you are looking through a new mind, but for the sake of wisdom, we are going to do one more thing as a means of pure protection. I am going to ask you to **look out.**

God's Word teaches the principle of there being strength in numbers and that we are meant to live out this life in community with fellow believers. How do you see that in Ecclesiastes 4:9-12 and James 5:16?

I have found that accountability can make all the difference in my life, especially when I am in battle. In order for you to protect your freedom, I am highly recommending that you find yourself an accountability partner. Ideally, this is someone who is the same sex, more spiritually mature than you, can ask you the tough questions, and will follow through on their commitment to hold you to your renewed mind. Accountability and checking in from time to time with another Christ-follower keeps us on track and helps us to focus when it's so easy to get distracted. I find that my actions are more deliberate if I know I am liable to another believer. Support and encouragement is what God has always destined for His body to provide for one another--everybody needs a cheerleader! And if our freedom is worth it, then we are also willing to hear the needed confrontation from someone who cares about our freedom and doesn't want to see us enslaved again.

"Wounds from a sincere friend are better than many kisses from an enemy." Prov. 27:6 (NLT)

Your journey to freedom is now complete. It doesn't mean that you will never find yourself in bondage again, but now you will know what you need to do in order to become free in Christ again. You will...

LOOK BACK

    LOOK WITHIN

        LOOK UP

            LOOK THROUGH A NEW MIND

            LOOK OUT

Last Look in the Mirror

Who would you like to come alongside you in processing what is needed for true freedom in your life? Name one older, godly woman you could meet with to go over Days 11-16. _____

Would you commit to setting this up some time in the next two weeks? Y or N

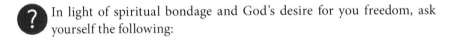 In light of spiritual bondage and God's desire for you freedom, ask yourself the following:

What stands out to you about God and His character today?

What is the one thing that you learned about yourself today?

How do these answers relate to your present life? What could they be saying to your mind, emotions, or will?

What is the one thing I can change/add/stop or continue growing in?

SPECIAL NOTE: Please don't hesitate to seek professional counseling or outside help for issues that you can't break free from or need help working through.

Freedom Is Worth Fighting For

His Spirit

What Freedom Needs

Do you remember that freedom is worth fighting for? It's worth taking the time right now, even though it feels like there are so many things you need to get done. This time with God is worth it--more than worth it. Stop and pray before you begin.

We have spent the last days looking at some of the huge, desolate landscapes that hold us in bondage--unpacked baggage, self-righteousness, fear, worry, and strongholds. God has warned you. You are no longer ignorant. He wants you to clearly see how unstable, ever-changing, unhealthy, destructive, deceptive, and evil these are. It is not that you won't ever be tempted to go there again, but He longs for you to experience the freedom He offers and relish in it. So much so, that when you find yourself tempted to carry some emotional baggage around, operate out of religious pride, be afraid, worry, or grant Satan a foothold, you recognize it and run!

If you have experienced a newfound freedom or have enjoyed freedom in the past, describe what it feels like and looks like to you. If you never have, describe what you imagine it to feel like and look like.

I love one of the pictures God uses to illustrate freedom--that of a calf kicking up his heels. Listen to what He says in Malachi 4:2:

"But for you who fear My Name, the Sun of Righteousness
will rise with healing in His wings. And you will go free,
leaping with joy like calves let out to pasture." (NLT)

"And you will go out and skip about like calves
released from the stall." (NASB)

"You will be bursting with energy, like colts frisky and frolicking." (MSG)

I was raised in a city neighborhood of California so I was clueless when it came to the life habits of farm animals. But when I married my husband, I moved into a small home adjacent to his parents' farm. Several times I had to cover chores for my in-laws when they would go to visit the Village Mission churches that they oversaw. One of my chores was to take care of the baby calves and bottle feed them. After being penned up in a stall, you should see a calf get to run out of the barn into the wide open farm land. Truly, those calves run around kicking and jumping as if they had been hog-tied and bound until that very moment. It is a sight to see. The frolicking calf so clearly parallels our release from the dark, cramped, stinky stall of sin out into the fresh air and green pasture of life with a new sense of freedom.

This kicking-up-your-heels kind of freedom only comes through the ministry of the Holy Spirit as we learn to surrender our self-driven lives to His control. Think about how God's Word has instructed us to battle our bondage: *"be transformed by the renewing of your minds"* (Romans 12:2), *"trying to please God versus man"* (Galatians 1:10), *"turning to perfect love to cast out fear"* (1 John 4:18), *"casting all your cares upon Him"* (1 Peter 5:7), *"bringing every thought captive to the obedience of Jesus Christ"* (2 Corinthians 10:5), *"trust in the Lord"* (Proverbs 3:5). That sounds like a list of "the impossible" for me-- which is exactly the point. It is impossible for me and it is impossible for you.

Freedom is only accessible through the power of the Holy Spirit. One of my favorite passages is (Ephesians 1:18-21) because it speaks about how the power that lives within us is the power that raised Christ from the dead. That is the power available to each woman, young or old, who has given her heart to be a Christ-follower. But how do we access that power? Does it get turned on and off? Do we push some hidden button in our Bibles? Do we say some special words? Or, perhaps, God does like He always does and chooses a way that builds our relationship with Him, causing us to draw closer.

 We can look at something and not even really see it. Please don't let that happen right now. Look intently at what God wants to reveal to you.

Looking in God's Mirror

Again, God has chosen an amazing word picture to illustrate one of His critical truths--being controlled by the Holy Spirit is like being drunk on the Holy Spirit. Coming from an alcoholic family, I can tell you one thing for sure because I've witnessed it time and time again: You will do things drunk that you would never do sober. Did you get that? You will do things drunk that you would never do if you were sober. Why is that? It's because you are no longer in control. Your reflexes have been delayed and your impulses have been given free reign. With each drink, you lose a small portion of your control and the alcohol gains that portion. Eventually a line has been crossed and you are no longer in control, the alcohol is.

Can you recall a time when you did something that you thought you would never do? What was it and what do you think was 'in control' of you? (alcohol, fear, desire to belong, need to be loved, etc.)

It can be a frightening thought to have something else have more power over you than your own will. That is actually what kept me from turning to alcohol or drugs in my deepest pain and time of need--I was terrified of something else being in control of me that I couldn't trust. Then I met Jesus, a Savior who only wants God's glory and my best. He has proven Himself to be trustworthy over and over in my life. When His Spirit is in control, I am at peace. When His Spirit is in control, there is a supernatural power at work within me, leading me to freedom.

Let's back up this bus for a minute: Before we can be filled with the Holy Spirit, we need to understand that...

First, We are Indwelt by the Holy Spirit

When we began a relationship with Jesus Christ, at the very moment we agreed with His substitutionary death on our behalf and surrendered our sinful will to Him as Lord, we were indwelt by the Holy Spirit and His power became ours. His coming to live inside of us is a once-for-all deal. (John 7:37-39; 1 Corinthians 6:19; Romans 5:5; Romans 8:9)

What do 2 Corinthians 1:22, Ephesians 1:13, and 4:30 say about God sealing you with His Holy Spirit?

How would you explain what it means to be sealed by the Holy Spirit?

The word "sealed" is used in Matthew 27:66, referencing Christ's tomb being sealed. In Romans 4:11, the word "sealed" is talking about circumcision being a sign and seal of righteousness. And, in Revelation 7:3, the word "sealed" is in reference to when the foreheads of believers receive a seal to protect them from the upcoming wrath. John Piper looks at all three passages and states the definition this way, "God sends the Holy Spirit as a preserving seal to lock in our faith, as an authenticating seal to validate our sonship, and as a protecting seal to keep out destructive forces. The point is that God wants us to feel secure and safe in his love and power." [1]

Fellow sister in Christ, if you are His, then know that you have the Holy Spirit living within you and you should be completely secure in that "sealed" humbling truth.

Then Begins the War for Control:

The Flesh (You) or the Holy Spirit

What can you learn about the battle for control in these verses?

Romans 6:11-13

Romans 7:18-23

Romans 12:21

Galatians 5:16-18

God says in Galatians, Ephesians, and Acts that we are to be filled with the Spirit or controlled by the Spirit. Some of you might have thought, "Didn't that happen at salvation? And, if it did, then why is He commanding me to keep doing this?" The indwelling of His Spirit happens once, but according to all these other times, the tense of the Greek verb conveys an ongoing concept when it comes to being controlled, full of, or filled with the Holy Spirit. ("Filling" and "Controlled" are interchangeable terms--both carry the idea of relinquishing control.)

When the Holy Spirit indwells us at salvation, an irreconcilable war begins! The flesh versus the Spirit! It is a 24-hour a day and 7 day a week battle. Thus the question lies within this battle, "Who will be in control?"

Who will be in control for the day? Who will be in control this hour? God longs for us to be Spirit-controlled at all times. Why do you think that is? Here are just a few reasons:

You can live freely.
You are smack dab in the middle of God's will.
You look more like Jesus.
It means you are listening to Him versus telling Him.
You have joy.
You have courage and supernatural boldness.
You can patiently wait.
Peace will rule your heart and mind.
Your heart is softened with kindness and compassion.
You are given the ability to persevere.
You do good things.
Your love draws others.
You find self-control.
Your faith deepens.
You now are able to bring Him the glory that belongs to Him alone.

Wouldn't you think that we would all long for the Holy Spirit to be in control? That we would do whatever it took to experience His fullness? One would think.

You might be wondering at this point, "So what if I do want to walk in the Spirit and live a Spirit-controlled life? How do I do that?" I am going to stay with God's word picture of being drunk with His Spirit and simplify it into two steps: #1- Admit you are a sinaholic and #2 - Hand over the keys. (Remember that being drunk with His Spirit is a good thing.)

Admit you are a Sinaholic

My cousin Carol is a recovering alcoholic who loves to speak on panels in the high schools. She knows her steps for her recovery process and she will be the first to tell you that the first step is the most critical--Admit you are powerless over____(sin)____ and that your life has become unmanageable. This is the total, unrestricted acceptance that you cannot conquer sin on your own. No matter how hard you try, how long you fight it, or how many people you surround yourself with, you humbly acknowledge that fighting sin is outside of your capability and left to yourself, you will choose sin every time.

Where can your flesh take you according to Galatians 5:16-26?

I love how The Message states it:
> "*It is obvious what kind of life develops out of trying to get your own way all the time: repetitive, loveless, cheap sex; a stinking accumulation of mental and emotional garbage; frenzied and joyless grabs for happiness; trinket gods; magic-show religion; paranoid loneliness; cutthroat competition; all-consuming-yet-never-satisfied wants; a brutal temper; an impotence to love or be loved; divided homes and divided lives; small-minded and lopsided pursuits; the vicious habit of depersonalizing everyone into a rival; uncontrolled and uncontrollable addictions; ugly parodies of community. I could go on.*" Gal.5:19-21

The flesh is our natural tendency and our natural tendency is to sin. So we need to daily, hourly, moment by moment admit that we need help, that we cannot do it, that we are powerless. Like a friend of mine teaches, this admission is not like "throwing in the white towel" at a boxing ring. It is not like "waving the white flag" signaling a surrender in the midst of a battle. It is about relinquishing control. You choose to relinquish your emotions, your will, and your reason. It is emptying yourself of yourself.

Why do you think you hold onto the deception that you can do it yourself? Where do you think that comes from?

Can you recall a time when you were unsuccessful at managing your life? How did you feel about the outcome? Who was affected by it and how?

I imagine that my life each day is like a clear, glass cup that is automatically filled with the water of me when I awake each morning: I am then given the choice to either live that day out filled up with myself or to take a moment to pour myself out of the cup--to empty myself of Christie--and declare that I don't want my selfishness, my pride, my impatience, my need for control, my manipulation, my worry, my concerns, etc. to be in control that day. I recognize that if I am filled with me, then I am setting myself up for a day of self-centered, unprotected chaos.

Hand Over the Keys

Once you have emptied yourself of you, which relinquishes control, it is time to determine who or what you want to give that control to for the day. There are a million options out there, but only One you can wholeheartedly trust. You need to decisively ask the Holy Spirit to take over, since He is the only One who knows the will of God and will always steer you towards His glory. So the control of each day is like driving a car, and the choice lies with you as to who gets the key--you or the Holy Spirit?

Many Christians think this is just automatically done, but God's Word teaches us that it is our choice to *"walk in the Spirit,"* (Galatians 5:16) or *"be filled with the spirit."* (Ephesians 5:18) God has given us the choice to drive ourselves or to hand the keys over to His Spirit. Your cup that is emptied each morning is then filled with the Spirit when you give Him the keys.

We need to daily (for me, sometimes hourly) and intentionally get out of the driver's seat and hand over the keys to the Spirit so He can determine where we go that day, how fast we are going to go to get there, the route we are going to take, whether we need to stop along the way, etc. The funny (and sad) thing is that so many times I have given Him the keys and once I see where I think He is headed, I shout, "Oh, I know how to get there! I think I'll drive now because I know a shortcut," and I grab the keys back, right out of His Hand. You see, we can give the Spirit some control but not all. If we were to be honest with ourselves, we know when we are holding back and how much more we need to let go of before He is driving again. Just like with alcohol, those who drink know how many drinks they can consume before they are no longer in control.

Sadly, each of us can also be a horrible backseat driver. Perhaps we haven't taken the key back and hopped into the driving seat, but we might as well have because we can be heard (quite easily in fact) complaining about how slow He is going, about how He really doesn't know much about today's traffic laws, or about how He could use a little help from Mapquest. We have non-stop suggestions for the changes He needs to make. Can you imagine how He tires of hearing all of our input that implies He is clueless? Can you envision the young woman saying to the Creator of the Universe that she knows better?

What keeps you from giving up control to the Holy Spirit in your life? Why is it hard for you to hand over the keys?

Recall a time when you gave Him control. What did that feel like? How did it turn out? Who was affected and how?

Each day, we need to admit we are sinaholics who will make a mess out of our lives if left in control and empty ourselves of us. Then we need to choose to hand over the keys to the One who is completely trustworthy and allow Him to sit in the driver's seat of our day.

Write your own prayer of what this could sound like each day. I will start it for you.

Good morning God. My name is _____ and I am a sinaholic ....

FUN IDEA: At times in my life, I have taken an old key and put it on a ribbon/string and worn it like a necklace, but under my clothes, as a private reminder of "Christie, who is driving your car?"

One more time, listen to the freedom and the fruit that comes from living with the Holy Spirit in control.

"But what happens when we live God's way? He brings gifts into our lives, much the same way that fruit appears in an orchard--things like affection for others, exuberance about life, serenity. We develop a willingness to stick with things, a sense of compassion in the heart, and a conviction that a basic holiness permeates things and people. We find ourselves involved in loyal commitments, not needing to force our way in life, able to marshal and direct our energies wisely." Gal.5:22-23 (MSG)

Last Look in the Mirror

In light of freedom needing His Spirit, ask yourself the following:

What stands out to you about God and His character today?

What is the one thing that you learned about yourself today?

How do these answers relate to your present life? What could they be saying to your mind, emotions, or will?

What is the one thing I can change/add/stop or continue growing in?

[1] Piper, John. "Sealed by the Spirit to the Day of Redemption." *Desiring God*. N.p., 6 May 1984. Web. 17 Aug. 2012. <http://www.desiringgod.org/resource-library/sermons/sealed-by-the-spirit-to-the-day-of-redemption?lang=en>.

Freedom Is Worth Fighting For

His Truth

What Freedom Needs

I hope you are in one of your favorite places to meet with Jesus today. Relax and thoroughly enjoy this time together. Don't miss His smile for you or His eagerness to share His heart in His word.

Yesterday, we spent time allowing God to reveal to us that without His Holy Spirit there can be no freedom. We must have His power for we cannot do it alone. We are sinaholics who need to admit our powerlessness and hand over our keys of control to Him daily, sometimes moment by moment.

Today we are asking God to teach us another "must have" for His freedom. We "must have" His Spirit and we "must have" the power of His truth at work in our hearts and minds. Unfortunately, we have many misconceptions about truth that rob us from experiencing the life-changing truth that sets us free.

Let me list a couple of the lies about truth and please place a check mark in front of either of these that you have bought into:

_____ Truth is subjective--it changes with each person's tastes, feelings, and perspective. "What your truth is might be completely different than my truth."

_____ Truth is situational--it changes according to the individual situation or context.

"Truth of today may not be the truth of tomorrow given a different environment."

I beg you to never buy into one of these lies that will give an open invitation to Satan to bring about dark bondage or wreak havoc in your life. Please know that truth is absolute-- unalterable and permanent. Truth is objective--the same for all people. And, most importantly, we come to truth to adjust our lives and hearts and minds. We see the falsehoods we have bought into and we make the necessary changes--**Truth Never Budges.**

John 14:6 - Truth is Jesus Christ.
Hebrews 13:8 - Jesus Christ is the same yesterday, today, and tomorrow.

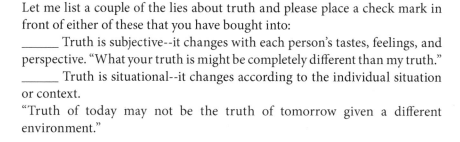 Pause now and ask God to reveal His truth to you today and to make it easy to understand. Ask Him to allow you to have a few "wow" moments and to be willing to make any necessary changes that you might need to make.

Your Thoughts Please

Why do you think that you would need truth in order to experience freedom?

What do you think are some of the benefits of a truth that is absolute and objective?

How do you feel about a truth that asks you to adjust your life to its standards and not the other way around?

Our thoughts and perspectives and feelings are always important, but they must be sifted through and held up to the light of God's truth at all times. His Word is always the final word.

Looking in God's Mirror

Experiencing the Goal of Truth in Your Life

The goal of God's truth is crystal clear: you know His truth and His truth sets you _____ ! (John 8:31-32)

There is a key concept to grasp from these verses. The Greek word translated "know" is *ginōskō*, and it carries the idea of knowledge that comes from personal experience. In the Old Testament, the word know is used to describe sexual relations between a man and a woman, as in Adam knew Eve. Therefore, *ginōskō* implies an intimate knowledge of a person or a thing that is born out of experience.

In *A Study of the Bible* by Peter Giardina, he observes the following:
   Note that the above passage tells us it is His disciples, those who abide in His word, who shall know the truth in this experiential manner. The verb "abide" means to act in accordance with. Hence, those who experience Jesus' word, and act in accordance with it (being obedient and not disobedient like Adam and Eve) will understand the truth, and their experiential knowledge (ginōskō) will make them free. Memorizing Bible verses and passages is a splendid and worthwhile activity. However, committing the truth to memory will not free us from the prison of sin. This only happens when we know His truth intimately...experientially...when we attain understanding. We must take a bite of the truth and swallow it...make it a part of us...become one with it...gain an experiential knowledge of it...then we will be made free. This is true freedom. [1]

I love how Mr. Giardina compares experiencing truth to taking a bite out of it, swallowing it, and becoming one with it. I think I put truth on a plate at the beginning of my walk with Christ and just studied it. Then, for many years, I allowed others to chew on God's Word and serve me their chewed-up, spit-out food. Now I know, firsthand, the satisfaction of feasting on His truth for myself. I know the sweet taste of believing every morsel of it, allowing it to continue to give me nutrition as I meditate on it, and the incredible freedom that comes from putting its nourishing strength into practice!

Experiencing the Role of Truth in Your Life

God never intended the book of His truth to be about information that we needed to learn, and by somehow having this information stored up in our brains, our lives would be changed. No! God gave us the gift of His Bible to transform our very hearts and minds, and it is within the transformation that we experience the agent of change that leads us to true freedom.

If we desire freedom, then we will not merely study the role of truth in our lives. We will come to God's Word and ask ourselves whether we are experiencing these truths found in 2 Timothy 3:16-17.

Read 2 Timothy 3:16-17 aloud--then read it one more time, slowly digesting the words.

(1) God is asking you and He is asking me if we are experiencing that *Truth is God-breathed*--Are you?

If we desire freedom then we know that every time we open God's Word and begin to read, He is breathing upon each word or breathing every thought into our soul. This may sound funny to you, but I ask to feel His breath. I thought about intimate conversation with my husband and how there are times we are close enough to one another that I can feel Mark's breath on me as he talks to me, and I want that same experience with my Savior. This is why God's Word is so profitable--it is God-given and God-breathed. Every jot and every tittle (the smallest strokes made with a writing utensil) is straight from the mouth of God. There is nothing in the Scriptures included by chance.

Are you living in such a way that you treasure the truth in God's Word? Do you search for the value in every paragraph? Does the priority you place on your time with God in His Word reflect that it is a treasure?

Breathing and breath are also an indicator of life, of the living. This is my favorite part of God's truth...it is alive. I have experienced this countless times in my 30-plus years of walking with Him. I can read a passage that I have read many times before, I can read a chapter that I have studied and heard several sermons on, or I can be sitting in Bible study discussing a portion of Scripture that I have already prepared for and God will make a brand new truth come alive to me that I have never noticed or seen or heard before! I think to myself "how can that be?"

Towards the end of every year, I ask God to lead me to a section of His Word to base all my goals on for the upcoming year. Once chosen, I will spend the first day of each month reading those particular verses in a different version. I never ceased to be blown away that God reveals something new and alive and different to me each month--just think about it--that is twelve different messages for my heart from the exact same passage twelve months in a row! Oh, how I love His law. His Word is living, with fresh breath for each time we want to come aside and spend time feasting on His truth.

Take a moment now to thank Him that His truth is alive and ask Him to really make that real to you in this upcoming year.

(2) God is asking you and He is asking me if we are experiencing the *Teaching of His Truth*--Are you?

If we desire freedom then we know that the only path to wisdom is through His truth and so we choose to become wisdom seekers. We are ready to put our big girl panties on paired with some heavy duty hiking boots so that we can search out, study, dig into, and even roll around in God's Word. We know it will get dirty--even messy--because we will have questions, things we don't understand, truth we aren't quite ready to hear, and more, but that doesn't stop our quest from gaining understanding of God and His will. That doesn't squelch our desire to keep being pointed towards Christ until He returns. That doesn't deter us from our relentless pursuit of wisdom.

Ponder and answer: Do you also study, not solely read, God's Word? You know the difference (just imagine reading a novel versus studying for your World History exam). How often do you meditate on one of His truths--kind of like a cow chewing on its cud where it regurgitates it over and over in order to keep chewing? Do you have any verses or portions memorized so that the Holy Spirit can bring them to your mind quickly when faced with the temptation to sin?

One of the greatest benefits of going to Bible College for me was that I graduated with this amazing foundation of truth that acted as my standard for all of life. Granted, I am daily adding to this grid making it more solid and extensive, but experiencing the teaching of truth gives you a sieve to sift through all of life's questions, choices, considerations, convictions, and decisions. What an invaluable tool for the wise woman who wants to be free!

Take a moment to thank God that He hasn't made your life a mystery to be solved but He has given you the truth you need for understanding and wisdom.

(3) God is asking you and He is asking me if we are experiencing the *Conviction of His Truth*--Are you?

God showing us what is wrong in our lives is just as much of a gift as it is for a loving father to give consequences for bad choices. Can you imagine if God allowed us to just keep making horrible choices that would bring even worse consequences? If He just kept letting us walk down a dead end street that would lead to scars we can't imagine, if He just let us mosey our way into quick sand that could kill us, what kind of love is that? The answer is that it isn't love at all. God blesses us with the truth of rebuke.

I love teaching on the truth found in 2 Corinthians 7:10:
> *"Godly sorrow brings repentance that leads to salvation and leaves no regret, but worldly sorrow brings death."*

Simply put, guilt is from God and it is good, while shame is from Satan and it is bad. Healthy guilt produces repentance as it exposes our sin and our rebellion. It causes us to fall at the foot of the Cross pleading our need for forgiveness, and our need for God Himself. Once released from the guilt, we are free to move forward without regret, like the verse states. Our guilt led us to our rescue from that sin, and implants the reminder of our need for our Savior. Whereas, Satan would love for us to wallow in our shame, to swim in a whirlpool of self-centeredness for an endless amount of time. Shame is terribly unhealthy as it immobilizes us and begs us to remain stagnant, leading to a slow hardening of our soft heart.

Haven't you seen firsthand what happens when convictions aren't taken to heart? Don't you wish your family would be convicted to talk about the giant elephants in the room that are causing everybody to act immaturely? Don't you ever wonder how your life would be different if you had responded to the conviction of truth sooner? What traps could have been avoided if you had paid heed to His truth the first time?

Please note a stern warning when it comes to conviction. As women, both young and old, it is very easy for us to usurp the role of the Holy Spirit and see it as our responsibility to convict others of their sin. That is not our job--never has been and never will be. Women are not called to put on their own version of the truth costume and try to ask questions that will bring conviction or remind someone of something he/she should feel guilty about or sigh in such a way that we communicate one should be feeling remorse. We are not part of the Trinity, so let's give God's Word the power to bring conviction to others.

Take a moment now to thank God that He protects you with His conviction and that when His truth makes you feel guilty, it is a gift.

(4) God is asking you and He is asking me if we are experiencing the *Correction of His Truth*--Are you?

Our incredible God doesn't use His truth to convict us and then just leave us to ourselves forgiven, yet still wondering how on earth we are supposed to get it right next time. No, God also uses His truth to set things right, and to restore us by showing us the right way to live.

Barnes Notes on the Bible says:
   Man needs not only to be made acquainted with truth, to be convinced of his error, and to be reformed; but he needs to be taught what is right, or what is required of him, in order that he may lead a holy life. He should be followed with the principles of the word of God, to show him how he may lead an upright life. The Scriptures furnish the rules of holy living in abundance, and thus they are adapted to the whole work of recovering man, and of guiding him to heaven. [2]

If we desire freedom, then after we are convicted, we will seek out correction. We will ask Him to show us the right way to live, the proper attitude to have next time, and the pure motive we want to cultivate in our hearts. Freedom comes from the realization that your relationship with Jesus Christ is far more about the do's than it is about the don'ts. You experience this freedom when becoming more Christ-like becomes your focus. You start asking yourself, "What am I doing for my Messiah? Who am I becoming? How can I walk the narrow path next time?" The truth of His correction will always illuminate the way ahead.

Take a moment to thank God for being so concerned about your heart that He will never leave you hanging. He will correct you and show you how to reflect His Son.

(5) God is asking you and He is asking me if we are experiencing the *Equipping of His Truth*--**Are you?**

If you desire freedom, then you are witness to how His truth equips you for every good work that He calls you to. Truth matures the believer, no longer relying on milk alone to nourish your relationship, but moving onto more solid foods. Through the truth of His Word, we are put together and shaped for each task He has for us. I know that there have been countless times He has prepared me in His word for something that was just around the corner even though I was ignorant to it at the time. Because I journal, I have been blessed to go back and be able to say, "Wow! You made me ready."

Let me clarify though, I don't believe that truth is meant just for you and your life. That would be pretty self-serving. I believe we are called to bear the truth that we learn to everyone in our world.

Are you a truthgiver to those around you? Have you considered that our Lord might want to equip another brother or sister by your sharing of the truth He has given you? Are you constantly pointing others to God and His truth?

Take a moment to thank God that He equips you through His truth--that He never asks you to do something that He won't give you the skills or understanding or strength for.

(6) God is asking you and He is asking me if we are experiencing the *Completion of His Truth*--**Are you?**

To know freedom is to know that you cannot add to or take away from God's truth. You know beyond a shadow of a doubt that His Word is complete, no embellishing is needed. You aren't searching outside of His truth for any answers or input or knowledge or guidance or reference. You know that Truth stands alone and you embrace it. You can say with complete conviction that you don't need more truth or deeper truth than what is written between the first words in Genesis and the last words in the book of Revelation.

Take a moment to thank God that His truth is complete and ask Him to settle this in your heart once and for all.

God's Warning: People Will Turn From the Truth

Read 2 Timothy 3:1-5 and list all the things that turning away from truth will bring into your life.

What will you do to make sure that you never turn from Truth?

Looking in Your Mirror

Evaluate where you are and aren't experiencing truth in your life by rating each area on a scale from 1-10. (1 is not experiencing truth at all and 10 is experiencing truth in abundance.)

Truth is God-breathed _____
Truth is a Teacher _____
Truth is a Convicter _____
Truth is a Corrector _____
Truth Equips Us _____
Truth is All We Need _____

Are you currently walking away from any truth? Compromising any truth? Denying any truth?

Sister, God's truth never budges. Do you realize that means it is 100 percent solid, 100 percent secure and 100 percent able to transform your life from the inside out?

Last Look in the Mirror

In light of the truth setting you free, ask yourself the following:

What stands out to you about God and His character today?

What is the one thing that you learned about yourself today?

How do these answers relate to your present life? What could they be saying to your mind, emotions, or will?

What is the one thing I can change/add/stop or continue growing in?

Beautiful lady, today I am asking God to give you a deeper desire for His truth.

[1]   Peter, Giardina. "A Study of the Bible." *The More Sure Word*. Wordpress.com, n. d. Web. Web. 16 Jan. 2013.

[2]   Barnes, Albert. "Barnes Notes on the bibles." *Biblos*. N.p., n.d. Web. 16 Jan 2013. <Biblos.com>.

Freedom Is Worth Fighting For

Freed to Love

Where Freedom Leads

There is something good around the corner--a special blessing that God has just for you this day. Let go of everything else right now and pray for eyes to see it and ears to hear it.

Empty Versus Full

Describe how your stomach feels when it feels empty and when it feels full.

Describe how your heart feels when it feels empty and when it feels full.

We will come back to this in a bit.

Get Yoked!?! Trading the Emptiness for the Fullness

Today we venture into the world of agriculture and farming equipment to understand God's teaching more deeply. A common tool for the farmer is the yoke--the bar of wood that unites two animals (usually oxen) enabling them to work in the fields more effectively, draw loads more easily, and pull instruments for greater production.

When you are yoked with Satan and sin, you are dragged everywhere they go, and both Satan and sin love the darkness, death, and chaos. Theirs is a heavy yoke to bear and it is crafted out of your emptiness. You will be a pawn used by him in his wicked schemes, and you will unknowingly advance his doomed battle plan for the Throne.

When you are yoked with Christ Jesus, you are blessed to accompany Him everywhere He goes, and He loves the light, life, hope, and peace. His yoke is easy; crafted out of His fullness. You will not find life easier *per se,* but you will find it far more productive and effective for eternity's sake as your Savior shares your journey alongside of you. In addition, you will be on the Victor's side in the final battle.

 Now that we have an understanding of our choices of yokes in life, we can move forward with God's message that He has for us in Galatians 5.

Looking in God's Mirror

Read and write out Galatians 5:1 in your own words.

Paul starts out this chapter with a reminder of the foundational truth in the Christian life: "You were called to freedom!" Precious one, you have been called to get out of the yoke of slavery to sin as fast as you possibly can and hightail it over to Christ's yoke of freedom. Wait a minute--it seems like an oxymoron doesn't it? We break the bondage of one yoke in order to willingly place ourselves under another yoke? And that's freedom? Wouldn't freedom be the option of "no yoke at all?" The truth is that there is no such thing as "no yoke at all." Remember that you were born under the yoke of the Law--God's requirements for one to be considered righteous.

Paul in Galatians 5:1 and Peter in Acts 15:10 talk about yoke of bondage that the Law brings, the yoke that no one can carry. The requirements of the Law are beyond our capacity! No human has ever been able to keep God's Law. No human being has ever been able to keep even the Ten Commandments, especially after Jesus preached the true meaning of lust being even the thoughts in our mind and murder being even the anger in our hearts (Matthew 5-7)! In Romans 8:2, we are told *"through Christ Jesus, the law of spirit has set me free from the law of sin and death."* In other words, Christ Jesus has set us free from the yoke of bondage through the Law. Jesus took upon himself the yoke of Law and fulfilled it. Therefore, through Him we can be set free from the yoke of sin and death.

Dearest sister, what appears to be an oxymoron is not. Choosing to remove the yoke of Satan and sin and choosing, instead, to be yoked with Christ is the only way to experience continued freedom. Jesus offers all who are under the yoke of Law or sin the true rest for their souls.

> *"Come to me all you who are weary and burdened, and I will give you rest. Take my yoke upon you and learn from me, for I am gentle and humble in heart, and you will find rest for your souls. For my yoke is easy and my burden is light."* Matthew 11:28-30

Now, here's one of the many cool things about your freedom while yoked with Christ-- you are freed to love! Let's turn to verses 13-15 in the fifth chapter of Galatians.

> *"You, my brothers and sisters, were called to be free. But do not use your freedom to indulge the flesh; rather, serve one another humbly in love. For the entire law is fulfilled in keeping this one command: "Love your neighbor as yourself." If you bite and devour each other, watch out or you will be destroyed by each other.*

Now You are Freed to Love

Let's take these verses apart and really chew on them today.

"But do not use your freedom to indulge the flesh."

God gives us a warning here and He doesn't form it as an option, but as a command--"Do not." As a mother, those are very strong words when I am directing my kids. I feel like I have made myself crystal clear when I say the words "Do not."

Why do you think God commands us not to use our freedom to indulge our own flesh?

When I stop to think about God's commands for me, I am usually completely baffled again by His love. Did you catch it? He doesn't want us to turn right back around and find ourselves in bondage, yoked with Satan and sin again. We will have found our freedom only to lose it again--how tragic!

What sin tempts you the most to indulge in your own flesh? (Private - not to be shared)

"*Rather, serve one another humbly in love.*"

Here is our second command and I can't help but wonder, why do I need to be free in order to show love to others? Can't I give love whether I am enslaved or free? Spread love whether I am yoked with Satan or with Jesus? It seems not.

Here is where we will go back to where we started--how it feels to be empty and how it feels to be full. When we are captives to sin and yoked with our enemy, we are motivated by the emptiness within ourselves--the cravings, the rumblings, the holes, and the lostness. It is the surest sign that we are in the mode of searching for fulfillment and satisfaction. I have said for years that sin is every thought and action flowing out of a heart that is not allowing Christ to satisfy it. A soul that isn't being filled by the Lord will go into search mode for other filling options. When one is empty and searching, one cannot give love according to love's true definition.

Take a moment and list the characteristics of authentic love from 1 Corinthians13:4-8, 13.

Could your life live these truths out when you are empty, searching, and enslaved to sin?

Isn't that phenomenal how much God's Word makes complete sense when we understand what He was saying!?! I just can't get enough of His truth!

Listen to what John Piper, pastor and author, says concerning this: "When we love, we are not enslaved to use things or people to fill our emptiness. Love is the overflow of our fullness. Therefore, love is the only behavior that we can do in freedom. When God frees us from guilt and fear and greed and fills us with His all-satisfying presence, the only motive left is the joy of sharing our fullness. When God fills the emptiness of our heart with forgiveness and help and guidance and hope, He frees us from bondage to accumulate things and manipulate people." [1]

For the entire law is fulfilled in keeping this one command: "Love your neighbor as yourself."

Here is our third and, possibly, our most radical command--loving my neighbor as myself. This is how we have been called to express our fullness in Christ Jesus to others, not just loving them, but loving them in the same way we love ourselves. That's enough to knock me off of my feet.

Each human being is born with a deep-seated love of self that expresses itself in its self-preservation and self-seeking ways. This self-love motivates our lives, generates our energies, and provides our direction. For instance, true or false? You naturally jump out of the way if it looks like a car is going to hit you as you cross the road. That's self-preservation. Or consider the moments when, if you are honest with yourself, you really want to be first in line for food or want the exact piece of dessert that you like most. That's self-seeking.

So we are being commanded to take this self-love and turn it into others-love. It doesn't sound that bad until we actually put skin on it. It looks like this:

- As I make sure I get food when my stomach is growling, I will make sure my neighbor gets food when his/her stomach is growling.
- As I build a fire or turn on the heat to make sure my family is warm for the night, I will make sure that my neighbor has a house that is warm for his/her family for the night.
- As I shop for the perfect accessory for my new outfit, I will make sure that my neighbor has a great outfit too.

- As creatively as I celebrate the holidays and special occasions, I will make sure my neighbor's holidays and special occasions are done creatively as well.
- As hard as I work in pursuing my goals and dreams, I will work just as hard to make sure my neighbor is going after his/her goals and dreams.

That takes it to a whole different level of love, doesn't it? I write these words and examples with such deep conviction in my own heart of how much I fall short in truly loving my neighbor. And remember that when our Lord was asked, "Who is my neighbor?" Jesus replied, "Everyone." Read Luke 10:25-37 if you are not familiar with the parable of the Good Samaritan.

This kind of neighborly love can only happen supernaturally since we are naturally self-lovers. Here is one of the most important equations you should ever memorize:

$$\text{Self-Lover..... becomes a..... God-Lover..... leads to becoming an..... Other-Lover}$$

You cannot be an "other-lover" without first becoming a "God-lover." You need to be head-over-heels in love with God first. He needs to be first in your focus, first in your priorities of life, first in your thoughts, and first in your choices. That's why the first of the greatest commands is that you *"love the Lord our God with all your heart and with all your soul and with all your mind"* (Matthew 27:37). The second greatest command is to *"love your neighbor as yourself."*

Share the most recent time you were able to be an "other-lover" and the role God played in that experience.

"If you bite and devour each other, watch out or you will be destroyed by each other."

These verses conclude with our last warning. Relationships that don't serve one another in love, out of fullness from God Himself, will bring intense pain to each other and can easily be destroyed. We have to share love out of our fullness in Jesus, not out of our emptiness which causes us to act ravenously.

Most of us have experienced or watched relationships that just tear and rip at each other. It is tragic. It is sad. It is devastating. And it is not the way the body of Christ is called to live. Can you imagine the way the world would be blindsided by the Church if we truly loved our neighbor as ourselves? If we loved every person out of a heart and soul that was overflowing with the love of God?

How would your family or friends react if they witnessed this kind of love?

Looking in Your Mirror

How do you throw away your freedoms in Christ?

Why is sin's yoke so appealing to you?

When it comes to being deeply satisfied by God, if your heart were a gas tank, how full is it?

What areas of your soul still have holes? Name the holes or gaps that still cause pain or emptiness. (Optional sharing)

When you think of truly loving another as you love yourself, where do you do well and where do you become selfish?

What do you think God is specifically asking of you when it comes to loving your neighbor as yourself?

What "biting and devouring" relationship are you presently a part of? Are you the one biting or being bitten? What do you do about this?

Last Look in the Mirror

 In light of freedom leading to love, ask yourself the following:

What stands out to you about God and His character today?

What is the one thing that you learned about yourself today?

How do these answers relate to your present life? What could they be saying to your mind, emotions, or will?

 What is the one thing I can change/add/stop or continue growing in?

---

1   Piper, John. "Freed To Love." *Desiring God*. N.p., 12 June 1983. Web. 17 Feb. 2012. <http://www.desiringgod.org/resource-library/sermons/freed-to-love>.

Freedom Is Worth Fighting For

Freed to Bear Fruit

Where Freedom Leads

 Retreat for a short while today with your Savior and savor every moment. Prepare your heart now.

Well, we are going to hang out in the agricultural world for one more day because we are going to learn from God that we are given another amazing gift with our freedom--the gift of bearing fruit!

Women were created physically to bear a child, whether each one does or doesn't. She alone has the reproductive organs needed to reproduce, as well as the mammary glands to feed a child and the extra body fat needed to provide the fetus with enough nutrition.

Similarly, Christ-followers were created to spiritually bear fruit, whether each one does or doesn't. Christians alone have the Holy Spirit, and the Holy Spirit is needed in order to produce eternal fruit in one's life. Back in Galatians 5 we have been cheered on and scolded by Paul to remember that, "*It is for freedom that Christ has set us free,*" and that "*You, my brothers and sisters, were called to be free*" (vv. 1 & 13). Our freedom allows us to "*walk in the Spirit,*" and by "*walking in the Spirit,*" we will find fruit being produced in our lives (vv. 16 - 22).

Note: We covered what "*walking in the Spirit*" looks like on Day 17.

Read Galatians 5:1, 13-26. Note anything that you can learn about freedom and walking in the Spirit and bearing fruit of the Spirit.

There is an objective standard by which we can measure the vitality of our free relationship with Jesus Christ. Fruit is the telling sign. It is not simply one mark of a Spirit-filled life; it is the preeminent mark--the public testimony to a believer's sensitivity to and dependency on the Holy Spirit. That sensitivity is impossible when we are in bondage because we are buying into the father of lies and not listening to the Holy Spirit. That dependency on our God is impossible while we are yoked with our sin because we are looking to ourselves and the dead-end roads of sin to satisfy our emptiness. So, only in our freedom can we exhibit the fruit of His Spirit.

Quick Look in Your Mirror

If the fruit of the Spirit is a sure "sign" of your freedom because it originates out of the overflow of your intimacy with your God, then how bright is your "'sign" to others? In other words, do others see you as a fruit tree with...(circle the one that applies)

no apples   very few apples   some apples
lots of apples   apples falling off there are so many

Let's take a closer look at God's intention for us to be fruit-bearers in this life and the fruit of His Spirit.

Looking in God's Mirror

Created to Bear Fruit.

*"so that you may live a life worthy of the Lord and please
Him in every way: bearing fruit in every good work,
growing in the knowledge of God," Colossians 1:10*

No doubt that our Lord expects us to be productive in this earthly life, but He also makes it clear that the actual production of the fruit is by His Spirit alone. Only God can produce fruit. Our job is to abide in Him so that we can bear the fruit, hold it, and display it.

A man tells the following story, "Our neighbor had an apple tree, and I loved to sneak over and pluck an apple off its branches every once in a while. One day, I broke a little branch off the tree, took it to my backyard, plunked it down into the ground, watered it, and checked it daily for my own, convenient harvest of luscious apples. Those apples, of course, never came. I thought that the power to produce apples was in the little branch. But the branch only bore the fruit; it didn't produce the fruit. So long as it was severed from the tree, the branch could do nothing."

Likewise Jesus said, *"Remain in me, as I also remain in you. No branch can bear fruit by itself; it must remain in the vine. Neither can you bear fruit unless you remain in me. I am the vine; you are the branches. If you remain in me and I in you, you will bear much fruit; apart from me you can do nothing."* (John 15:4-5). To believe that someone could simply read through the fruit of the Spirit in Galatians 5 and then roll up their sleeves, dig their heels into the ground and conform to the list in their own power, would be the same as cutting a branch off the apple tree and believing it will produce apples. The fruit of the Holy Spirit cannot be produced in us apart from abiding in Jesus and walking in the Holy Spirit.

I once heard a sermon on "abiding in Christ" and the pastor explained the word abide as having a fuller meaning then just to remain in Jesus. He defined it as you making your home in Christ. You live within Him and are most comfortable there. You never have the intention of leaving. I think of it this way--He has become my new address!

How well are you abiding in the Vine? Is He your home? Day in and day out?
1   2   3   4   5   6   7   8   9   10

Is there something keeping you from feeling "at home" in Jesus?

Do you think you have come to believe that "apart from Him you can do nothing?" Does your life support that?

Fruit of the Spirit: Fruit Production

Read Galatians 5:22-23 again. Does it say "the fruit" of the Spirit OR "the fruits" of the Spirit?

Isn't that interesting? What is God trying to tell us here since He goes on to list what appears to be nine different kinds of fruit? According to the Greek, the word for fruit here in verse 22 is *karpos* and means fruit, harvest, and grain. But the choice to use the singular implies that the fruit comes as a whole package; there is unity. You don't go to the Holy Spirit grocery store and pick and choose what kind of fruit you want to exhibit today. Plain and simple, you are either walking in the Spirit and bearing the fruit of His character, or you aren't.

The world of agriculture reminds us that fruit production is not instant; it is a process. I know we live in a society that craves the instant and is constantly competing for who or what can do it faster, but our God doesn't operate according to culture. He operates according to His plan and His purposes. I believe He mostly chooses process over miraculously instant results because it is within the process that we draw closer to Him, and God is always in favor of that. So, as you learn to walk in the Spirit, you need to know that your fruit-bearing won't happen overnight, but it will be worth the wait.

Just imagine walking no further than your back yard to pick beautiful, crisp apples or plump, juicy plums. Fruit trees add beauty to any landscape and provide growers with delicious gifts of harvest each year. In order to flourish, fruit trees require consistent care and proper maintenance. Did you know that under the right conditions a single tree can produce fruit for up to 50 years straight? Now let's apply that to our lives.

Wouldn't you love for people to feel like they were walking through a bountiful orchard every time they were in your presence?   yes or no

Wouldn't you enjoy the feeling of consistent harvests in your life?   yes or no

And wouldn't you be thrilled to be able to look back and know that you faithfully bore fruit for your God for over 50 years?   yes or no

My heart is shouting a louder "yes" with each question!

Fruit of the Spirit: What Fruit Looks Like

Write out the 9 character qualities listed in verse 22 in groups of three as they appear.

Many believe that the unity of this list is also seen in the totality of character it represents. The first three are considered to be "upward" qualities that we find in our relationship with the Lord Himself. The second three are recognized as being "outward" qualities that we find in our relationship with others. The final three are regarded as "inward" qualities that develop within us. All are critical in every relationship we have and all are critical in reflecting our Messiah to a lost world.

Love - This is the kind of love that never fails and can be shown to those who don't love us in return--ouch! Human love has its limits; we can only give so much love. However God's love is unconditional, self-sacrificing and limitless. His love can be given through our surrendered spirits.

Who doesn't love you in return or who is exceptionally hard for you to love?

How could you let God love this person through you? Get specific.

Joy - This is not happiness dependent upon one's circumstances. This is joy that is a deep, abiding sense of delight in knowing God and is present in the midst of painful circumstances. Life can beat us up badly, but we can always ask for a new infusion of God's joy into our bruised souls.

When is it hardest for you to find joy--when you are hurting or when someone you love is hurting?

How do you seek God out for your joy when there is pain in your life?

Peace - This is an inner rest that comes from being in right relationship with your Almighty God. There are no walls or barriers between the two of you. It can even be felt when something you were counting on doesn't come through or when circumstances throw you an unexpected curve.

When was the last time you felt peace between you and God? What did you like the most about it?

Patience - This is longsuffering--you can wait when things aren't going fast enough for you. Why? Because you trust your God. Because you recognize that He is the One who has pushed the "pause" button of life. You know that He doesn't operate according to a calendar, but according to His greater purpose.

Is God the first place you turn when life isn't going according to your plan? Why or why not?

Kindness - This is tenderness toward those who treat you unkindly. It's the act of employing grace to prevent harsh reactions. it's the possession of His nurturing Spirit. Jesus wants to touch others with His kindness through you.

Would others call you a kind young woman? Why or why not?

Goodness - This is love in action and has an incredible drawing power inherent in it. It is character energized into acts of beneficence. It goes beyond good intentions. God tells us that we've been saved to fulfill the good works that He prepared in advance for us (Ephesians 2:10). Beth Moore puts it this way, "Goodness does."

Do you "do" for others? What enjoyment do you get from doing for others?

Faithfulness - This is you being true to a task and true to a relationship. If Jesus is your Bridegroom, then your heart is undivided. Your loyalty to Him is fierce. He can depend upon you without hesitation.

How faithful have you been this past month in your relationship with your Savior? How could you be more loyal?

Gentleness - This is a beautiful humility that softens the world around it. This gentleness stands for a life surrendered to God's real power. It doesn't believe that to give in is to lose, and it doesn't have a constant need to fight for its rights. It is a gracious strength that chooses to bow.

Which do you do more often--fight for your rights or choose to bow to God? Why?

Self-Control - Any woman is a valiant warrior who exhibits self-control. This is supernatural restraint from natural impulses and this is a critical component of victory. We live in a culture of entitlement and individual indulgence. To be able to say "no" to oneself is to close the door on things mastering you, and open the door to living fruitfully and freely.

Would you consider denying yourself something every day for one week? Try it. It could be coffee, shopping, or seconds at mealtime as an example.

I don't know about you, but my orchard has a long way to go to be the beautiful harvest that I want it to look like. But I am willing to put in the work because I want to display His splendor to this world. Let's be fruit-bearers for His Glory! Amen.

Last Look in the Mirror

 In light of bearing much fruit, ask yourself the following:

What stands out to you about God and His character today?

What is the one thing that you learned about yourself today?

How do these answers relate to your present life? What could they be saying to your mind, emotions, or will?

 What is the one thing I can change/add/stop or continue growing in?

WRAP UP TO YOUR FOURTH WEEK OF STUDY

Sweet sister, this week you saw pictured the two kinds of landscape in which we can live out our lives...one of barren waste or one of lush growth. You now know at least five different ways our Enemy captures us--through unpacked baggage, through fears, through worry, through self-righteousness, and through spiritual strongholds. However, none of those tactics hold greater power than what is at our fingertips--His Spirit and His truth. The choice is yours. You can choose to fight for freedom and live in freedom where you will find love and fruit or you can choose to stay and live in bondage where you will always be lied to and produce little to no fruit at all. Take it from a woman who has lived in both lands, and hear me as I scream in my loudest voice from the tallest tree, "I beg of you, do what you need to do to move to this land of freedom! It's worth fighting for!"

Surrender to His Spirit, grab His sword of truth, and claim the freedom that awaits you in Christ Jesus your Lord!

As Your Start Your Fifth Week of Study

I remember studying the Beatitudes in Matthew 5 for the first time. My Bible teacher pointed out the following observation, "You notice they are called the BEatItudes and not the DOatitudes. As Jesus began correcting the misconceptions about His kingdom, He made it clear that it is more about BEing than it is about DOing." I was struck by the truth that everything I do is actually born out of who I am!

Precious one, I believe Jesus is still pointing out the same message when it comes to impacting this world--how influential you are is more about who you are than it is about what you do.

Ask God to help you this week sincerely evaluate where you have been marked by Him, where you haven't, and how you are going to leave His mark on this world. Ask Him for a very special time together in these next five days.

INFLUENCE = LEAVING HIS MARK

DAY 21: Marked by Him: I Am Deeply In Love
Has God become all-consuming in your life yet?

DAY 22: Marked by Him: I Am A Wise Woman
Have you turned your back on folly and chosen to respond to wisdom's invitation?

DAY 23: Marked by Him: I Am A Woman Who Fears God
Do you understand God's commandment to fear Him, and do you desire more fear?

DAY 24: Marked by Him: I Am A Servant
Have you embraced God's standard of being His bondservant?

DAY 25: Marked by Him: I Am All About Bringing Him Glory:
Have you grasped God's supreme purpose for your life?

Leaving His Mark

Marked by Him

I Am Deeply In Love

You have a very important date right now--a date with the Lover of your soul--a date with the One who knows you best. Don't turn this time into speed dating. Relish these moments together and the difference they can make in your life.

We are about to study the last outcome of a woman who takes the time to look in God's Mirror of Truth and wrestles with what she sees about her God and herself--she will be a woman of Influence! The truth is that every woman is a woman of influence, whether she influences for the good or whether she influences for the bad. The real question to look in the mirror and ask yourself is, "What kind of influence do I want to be?"

According to one of my favorite authors, Dr. Henry Cloud, like a boat traveling through the water, every person leaves a "wake" behind them. I remember sitting in our ski boat and watching my favorite uncle jump back and forth over the wake as he waterskied. He thoroughly entertained us as kids. Similarly, the wake in your life and my life is the impact we leave behind as we interact with others. What is the nature of your wake? Are people laughing and waterskiing on your wake, feeling blessed and refreshed that you passed through? Or, are there people who feel like they've been run over, left bobbing in the water, sprayed or just ignored as you've gone by?

You are an influencer. What kind of impact do you want to have? What kind of imprint do you want to leave? As one of my best friends says, "Influence is based on your character, not on your position." First and foremost, your influence comes from who you are; and out of who you are, flows what you do.

Who you are originates with God Himself; it's all about *being* deeply in love with Him, *being* a wise woman, *being* a woman who fears Him, *being* His bondservant, and *being* all about bringing Him Glory! Then, the overflow of being marked by God Himself--being influenced by Him--pours out as you leave His mark everywhere you go and on everyone you come into contact with. So, this week we are going to study being marked by God Himself and what that should look like.

When I think of myself being "marked" by God, I can't help but think of tattoos and the permanence of their ink. The word tattoo comes from the Tahitian word *tattau*, which means "to mark," and was first mentioned in explorer James Cook's records from his 1769 expedition to the South Pacific. [1] Today, tattoos are professionally and artistically created by injecting ink into the skin. However, the fascinating part is that the tattoo is not in our epidermis, the top layer of skin that we see and the skin that gets replaced constantly. Instead the ink intermingles with cells in the dermis and shows through our epidermis. You see, the cells of the dermis are remarkably stable, so the tattoo's ink will last, with minor fading and dispersion, for your entire life!

Why do I go into this little "tattoo" teaching lesson? Because I do believe it has a great teaching point! Likewise, when we are "marked" by our God through His love, His wisdom, His Lordship, and His Glory, it goes far deeper than our first "heartskin's layer," which gets easily beat up and scraped by this world. God desires to "mark" us soul-deep! Soul-deep is where nothing in this world can touch His ink on us.

Listen to a friend of mine share her story.

I was on vacation with a friend, and at a point in my life when I wanted to turn my back on God. Too much pain...too hard...but I had a problem...I couldn't convince myself 100% that God didn't exist. If God existed and the Bible is true, then I had to live for Him...No turning back...No matter how hard. So as a reminder, my friend and I each got a cross tattoo on our shoulders. For me, it represented being marked for Jesus no matter what comes my way; the permanence of the tattoo a reminder that this is a "forever promise" commitment. No turning back. Here are some words of an old song that sums it up for me....

> *I have decided to follow Jesus, no turning back*
> *though none go with me, still I will follow*
> *this world's behind me, the cross before me*
> *even if I walk alone Lord, this I choose to do.*
> Lyrics by S. Sundar Singh, Public Domain

Tattoos received from an artist only serve as a reminder, while God's markings are transformational. I, personally, don't have any tattoos on my body nor do I plan on getting one, but I love the "heavenly ink" that God uses to keep marking my heart and soul.

If you've been marked by God Himself, then you are able to say..."**I am deeply in love with my God.**"

Quick Look in Your Mirror

What do you think are the top 3 things that today's young women...
IDOLIZE   SPEND $ ON   SPEND TIME ON?

I have often said that whatever you spend your time, money, and effort on is what you value. Likewise, whoever you spend your time, money, and effort on is who you value.

Look into the mirror of God's truth and see what Scripture says about where all of your affection, loyalty, and resources should be going. Then ask yourself the hard questions about whether your life reflects His truth.

Christie Rayburn

Looking in God's Mirror

Old Testament: Deeply in Love with God

What does your life look like if you have been marked by God with a deep love for Him that stands out from all other loves? Interestingly enough, the first truth that God gave His people was in the form of the 10 Commandments--not the "10 Suggestions" or "10 It-Would-Be-Really-Great-Ifs." God makes His priorities quite clear with His first four commandments being about our relationship with Him and the latter six having to do with our relationship with others. The first commandment sets the precedence of our loyalty in Exodus 20:2-3. Write out these two verses.

Surrounded by nations of polytheism, the worship of many gods, God was calling a people unto Himself alone. The Israel nation would be unique and set apart in the anchoring of fidelity to the One True God. Fast forward a few thousand years and God is still commanding us as Christ-followers to set ourselves apart from the philosophy of "many roads lead to heaven" and declare that we worship one God who claims to be the Only Way. Where does your loyalty lie?

God reminded His people in Exodus 20:2 that He brought them out of Egypt and out of slavery. Then before His breath finished, He commanded His exclusivity in our lives.

I believe He is reminding each of us that He alone delivered us out of our slavery to sin, out of our own Egypt. Has any other god delivered you from your sin? From your past? From your guilt? No! There is only One Redeemer, One Savior, One Messiah...and He reached down into your darkness and brought you into His Light. Your Deliverer deserves your allegiance and devotion. In fact, He commands it!

Read Exodus 20:4-6 and write out His second command.

The second command reveals that our God is jealous over our love for Him. It is not to be shared with meaningless idols. Every aspect of our worship is to be devoted to our Creator. He alone is in the spotlight of our adoration.

Read Isaiah 44:6-28 and list what you can learn about

GOD	IDOLS	IDOL WORSHIPPERS

Beth Moore, author and speaker, says, "Anything we try to put in a place where God belongs is an idol." [2] Israel lived in a culture where polytheism lent itself to the making of idols of all kinds, shapes, and sizes. The idols could be made of wood, metal, or stone, but each one was made by man. They could represent any animal, fish, bird, or form of a god and would be bowed down to by living men and women giving honor to a lifeless form. Now, we may think this ludicrous until we take a closer look at our own mirror.

How is my heart idolatrous? How do I give honor, adoration, or worship to something or someone other than God? Who or what do I exalt in my life? In simplest terms, let's start with how do you spend your money and your time? Who or what do you put effort towards? Who or what are you always talking about? Thinking about? I believe we can make idols out of anything or anyone--a boyfriend, an ipod, Facebook, music, sports, dancing, friends, parents, your car, your clothes and fashion, eating, TV, alcohol, smoking, video games, drugs, not eating, working out, your laptop, etc.

What have you been figuratively bowing down to in your life? Who have you idolized?

God is the only One who can satisfy every nook and cranny of our soul, but we often push Him out, deny Him His rightful place, or close ourselves off to His abundant grace. When we do this, we find ourselves with vacancies and voids in our heart, which will always lead to filling them with something that does not have the power, love, or ability to do what only Jesus can do.

Where are you vulnerable? What are your soul's nooks and crannies that you have not allowed God to fill?

You will always turn to some sort of an idol if you don't learn to turn to Christ Jesus for your every need. Philippians 4:19 reminds us of the rich truth that God will meet all of our needs through Jesus Himself.

You are deeply in love with God when you have no other gods before Him and you don't allow any idols to replace Him. You, too, are marked with possessiveness about the relationship you and your God share. Not that your loyalty or your worship doesn't ever waiver, but a steady growth in your love is what it looks like to be marked by Him.

New Testament: Deeply in Love with God

Now, I'd like us to listen to one more truth about how it looks to be marked by God as we keep falling deeper in love with Him. Let's go to Matthew 22:36-37 and write out the greatest commandment according to Christ Jesus.

If you are going to be a powerful influence for the eternal good, then you are going to live a life that screams to everybody around you that you *"love the Lord your God with all your heart, with all your soul, and with all your mind."*

With All Your Heart

In the Greek, the word for heart is *kardia*. It means the seat in the center of man's inward life--the place of human depravity or the sphere of divine influence. You are created to be influenced by God in the deepest part of who you are.

Read Ezekiel 36:26-27 and note what God tells you about your heart and how He wants to move you.

It was God's intention from the beginning to move us by His Spirit. Loving God with all our heart is about the inside of us. Remember Jesus' words to the Pharisees, the religious experts of the first century in Matthew 23:25-26, *"Woe to you, teachers of the law and Pharisees, you hypocrites! You clean the outside of the cup and dish, but inside they are full of greed and self- indulgence. Blind Pharisee! First clean the inside of the cup and dish, and then the outside also will be clean."* Jesus warned us about getting caught up in thinking that loving Him meant being concerned with the outside of us and how we behaved, while ignoring our hearts. He clearly instructed us that He was concerned with changing us from the inside out. He has given us a heart of flesh with which to love Him and His spirit to move us towards Him.

When it comes to your heart towards God, where does it fall on this scale?

Heart Of Stone   Heart Of Flesh

Do you seek God to change you from the inside out or do you try to change your heart by changing your outward actions first? _____ Which is more effective according to Scripture and why is that?

Loving God with all your heart is taking your new heart of flesh and trustingly placing it in the hands of God, asking Him to continuously do surgery to keep it soft, asking Him to make it beat for His name and His glory alone.

The following verse has become a prayer for my heart because I feel so far away from this kind of love: *"And besides You, I desire nothing on earth."* Psalms 73:25 (NASB)

Write out your prayer for your own heart and a deeper love for God.

With All Your Soul

The Greek word for soul is *psuche* and is used in a wide sense throughout the Bible regarding man's emotions, attitudes and will. From *psuche* we get the word "psychology," meaning the study of the soul. It literally means "the life we get from breathing." The soul is exposed in every breath we take. When Jesus commands us to love God with all our soul, He is saying to recognize His presence in every breath...it's a full time command! I may get overwhelmed with how huge that command is, but I just love the picture of every breath I exhale being filled with love for my Savior. Oh dear precious Lord, let it be so!

It is an exercising of the will (part of the soul) to love God in every life situation we face. Can you not see how it is much easier to breathe out love for God when life is going your way? And can you not relate to how it is much harder to exhale love for God with each breath when you feel like you are literally struggling for air to survive? My exhales have been known to be filled with anything but love at times. For it is in the storms of life that our soul's love for God is tested. When we are struggling, will we make the choice to love Him with the right actions and the right attitudes in spite of our choking, selfish emotions?

What was the last storm/trial/hard time you faced? Did you exhale love for God as you walked through it? If so, share how that felt. If not, share how you could have made different choices.

God warns us about taking our "soul love" for Him and trading it for the world. This is especially tempting to do when life gets hard or when we think the world has a whole lot more to offer us right now.

"What good will it be for someone to gain the whole world, yet forfeit their soul? Or what can anyone give in exchange for their soul?" Matthew 16:26

"Self-help is no help at all. Self-sacrifice is the way, my way, to saving yourself, your true self. What good would it do to get everything you want and lose you, the real you? What could you ever trade your soul for?" Mark 8:36 (MSG)

"And what do you benefit if you gain the whole world but are yourself lost or destroyed?" Luke 9:25

List 3 things that the world offers you and 3 things that God offers you instead:
The World Offers   God Offers

Sisters, this is an empty, dark world that can only offer vain things for the moment. Nothing this world has to offer can save you, forgive you, or bring you into eternity. Nothing this world offers can create in you a new heart, give you life, or touch your soul that was created to worship and love your Creator. Nothing this world has to offer can be counted on, is good, or will bring you security. Nothing this world has to offer can even come close to loving you the way the King of Kings does--unconditionally, sacrificially, and perfectly.

It's heartbreaking to think of the times I have given my soul to this world, that I have given this world my love and my choices and my attitudes. How foolish! May each of us wake up to the reality that we are commanded to love God with every breath, with all of our souls.

Take a moment to re-commit the breathing of your soul to God.

With All Your Mind

This Greek word for mind, *dianoia*, literally means "understanding." Our mind is our intellect--the place where knowledge and understanding are analyzed and manipulated to bring about a conclusion or decision. Loving God *"with all our mind"* means that everything we put in or allow in our minds is right, true and moral--that we align our conclusions and decisions based upon the commandments of God and the written Word of God in all situations. Remember how we talked about God's Word becoming the grid we sift all of life through?

How often are you basing your choices and decisions on the Word of God?
    Always   Usually   Occasionally   Seldom   Never

How often are you coming to conclusions about what you believe/value based on God's Word?
    Always   Usually   Occasionally   Seldom   Never

Which three do you allow or put into your mind the most and in what order?

God's Word	TV/Media	Parents' Beliefs
Magazines	Experts Thoughts	Other People's Opinions
Books	Friends' Voices	

The battleground for our love is not only fought in our hearts and souls, but in our minds as well. Our minds need to be *"transformed"* (Romans. 12:2), until we have the *"mind of Christ"* (Philippians 2). Our thoughts are what precede our actions. When you love God with all of your mind, you love "right thinking." Philippians 4:8 teaches us what right thinking looks like.

Read Philippians 4:8. If we love God, what are we to think on?

This list embodies what it means to live at the highest level of integrity, the highest level of morality, and the highest level of motivation. For you to live out this list means that your behavior doesn't contradict your thought life. This is a life that is true to people, to commitments, to promises, and to God. It is love that is free from falsehood.

How would others describe your relationship to integrity? Would they say you live free from falsehood?

Don't you just love the words "noble and right?" I think of a royal knight whose consistent choices of doing what is honorable over what is easy has made him worthy of respect. I think of the dignity that comes with taking the higher road in relationships and how it enables you to always carry your head held high. What is the focus of your thought life? More importantly, do your thoughts reflect your affection for your King?

How focused is your mind on nobility? On consistently doing what is most honorable?

Next come the words "pure, lovely, and admirable." There is nothing more attractive than that of moral purity. It is freshly alluring and captivating. You are promoting the holiness of God when you think on and live out His values. You love Him with your thoughts as you turn away from filth and vulgarity and foolishness. You are embracing His heart.

In the past three days, have your thoughts leaned more towards filth or purity? Why do you think that is?

Do you believe you are most attractive, most lovely, when you express God's character to others? Explain.

Lastly, think on what is "excellent or praiseworthy." We should esteem excellence and pursue it fervently, reflecting that our Lord is worth our efforts. We should recommend anything worthy of praise to others, and we should be practicing a lifestyle that would be noteworthy in commending the Lord we serve.

Please don't read that God commands our love to be perfect towards Him. When He commands our all He is showing us the direction we should be moving towards and growing in. Even as we struggle, our love for Him should always be marked by going deeper in some way. He is asking for all of our hearts, all of our souls, and all of our minds. He desires a soft, fleshy heart moved by His Spirit that chooses to breathe out love in spite of circumstances and keep its mind anchored on the truth of God's character.

If you are falling deeper in love with your Lord, then you have truly been marked by Him.

Last Look in the Mirror

 Reflecting on the depth of your love for God, ask yourself the following:

What stands out to you about God and His character today?

What is the one thing that you learned about yourself today?

How do these answers relate to your present life? What could they be saying to your mind, emotions, or will?

God has spoken to my heart. What is the one thing I can change/add/ stop or continue growing in?

Let's have a little fun this week. Don't be intimidated. You don't have to be an artist. It's just an opportunity for you to creatively put your reflections into picture form. If you were to get a tattoo reflecting your love for God, what would it look like? (Sketch it here.)

[1] Lohnes, Capt. Bret A.. "How Tattoos Work." *Tribal & Celtic Tattoos*. N.p., n.d. Web. 16 Jan 2013. <http://www.tribal-celtic-tattoo.com>.

[2] Moore, Beth. *Breaking Free: Making Liberty in Christ a Reality in Life*. Nashville, TN: B&H Publishing Group, 2000. 66. Print.

Leaving His Mark

Marked by Him

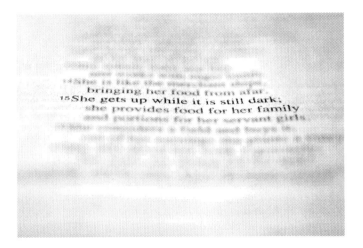

I Am A Wise Woman

 Wisdom cannot be hurried. So, pull up a chair and sit for a while. Glean.

Remember that we are asking ourselves what kind of influence do we want to be in the lives of others? What kind of impact do you want to have? Positive and powerful or negative and destructive? Your influence comes from who you are; and out of who you are, flows what you do. Who you are originates with God Himself; it's all about *being* deeply in love with Him, *being* a wise woman, *being* a woman who fears Him, *being* His bondservant, and *being* all about bringing Him glory! Then, the overflow of being marked by God Himself--being influenced by Him--pours out as you leave His mark in your world.

Fill in the blank from yesterday's study: If you've been marked by God Himself, then you are able to say, I am deeply _____.
Let's move onto the second distinction--If you've been marked by God, then you can say... **"I am a wise woman."**

How Wise Are You?

Test yourself and see how well you know some famous proverbs. (Answers at the end of today's study.)

A _____ in the hand is worth two in the _____.
Go to the ant, you sluggard, consider her ways and be _____.
A fool and his money are soon _____.
Can a man take fire in his lap without his clothes _____?
Actions speak louder than _____.
Spare the rod, _____ the _____.
Pride goes before destruction, a haughty spirit before a _____.
A man is known by the company he _____.
A gentle answer turns away _____, but a harsh word stirs up _____.
A friend in need is a friend _____.

These are considered famous words of wisdom and it's fun to see what we know off hand, but please be very clear about this--wisdom itself is not about knowing proverbs or knowing wise sayings. It is all about applying what you know to your life. Wisdom is a very active word.

Wisdom Versus Knowledge

Let's compare the two--knowledge versus wisdom. Knowledge can be defined as "information and skills acquired through experience or education; the theoretical or practical understanding of a subject." [1] Some synonyms for knowledge are learning, cognition, and science. On the other hand, Webster defines wisdom as "the quality of being wise; knowledge and the capacity to make use of it; knowledge of the best ends and the best means; discernment and judgment."[2] The critical difference being that wisdom goes beyond knowledge. Wisdom takes what is true or right and couples it with the action that needs to follow. Wisdom is not merely in your head, like knowledge; wisdom is lived out in your choices. Wisdom is knowledge with legs.

Many might compare wisdom to "taking the higher road," and most would agree that wisdom requires discernment, insight, prudence, and many times, self-control. (No wonder it's not easy to find a wise woman; it's not easy to be a wise woman.) Wisdom requires the hunger for the knowledge, the thirst for understanding it, and the commitment to live it out. But, oh how blessed is the wise woman!

Read from Proverbs 3 and circle the many blessings that come from wisdom:

> *Blessed are those who find wisdom, those who gain understanding,*
> *for she is more profitable than silver and yields better returns than gold.*
> *She is more precious than rubies; nothing you desire can compare with her.*
> *Long life is in her right hand; in her left hand are riches and honor.*
> *Her ways are pleasant ways, and all her paths are peace.*
> *She is a tree of life to those who take hold of her;*
> *those who hold her fast will be blessed.*
> *By wisdom the Lord laid the earth's foundations; by understanding*
> *he set the heavens in place; by his knowledge the watery*
> *depths were divided, and the clouds let drop the dew.*
> *My son, do not let wisdom and understanding out of your*
> *sight, preserve sound judgment and discretion;*
> Proverbs 3:13-21

We live in the days of vast amounts of knowledge literally available at the tip of our technological fingertips. This world is fast becoming an even playing field when it comes to gathering knowledge. A great deal of it through the internet and apps is available at no cost; knowledge is free. Wisdom, however, is something that is still priceless.

Now, here is one of the coolest things as a Christ-follower (we know there are a million cool things but just think of this as another one of the million)--"*If any of you lacks wisdom, he should ask God, who gives generously to all without finding fault, and it will be given to him*" (James 1:5). We can ask to be wise! Woohoo! I don't know about you, but I'm asking, and I'm asking for lots of it. (I'm thankful He didn't put a limit on how much we could ask for because I always feel like I need extra.)

 There is only one place to look for wisdom--God's Word. Dig deep. There is treasure waiting to be found.

Looking in God's Mirror

Seek Wisdom

It's time to get hungry for wisdom. We can't just want it. We can't just ask for it. Remember that wisdom is a word of action! We have to seek it. Are you ready to do your part? Roll up your sleeves and let's hear from God as to how much

He wants us to search after wisdom. You are about to be asked to be the Miss Indiana Jones of wisdom!

Read Proverbs 2:1-12. What is the purpose(s) of wisdom?

Record every verb from the above verses. Note that these are the actions God requires of you.

According to these verses in Chapter 2, list 5 benefits to your life to become wise.

Read Proverbs 4. What speaks to your heart to motivate you towards wisdom?

According to Proverbs 4: 7-9, (1) What does *at any cost* really mean? (2) Why should we gain wisdom at any cost? Why is wisdom that important?

Once you begin seeking for wisdom, like Indiana Jones searching for a lost treasure--with that kind of focus, intensity, purpose, and determination--then it is time to start applying what you have found. Remember, wisdom is a word of action!

Choose Wisdom: Wisdom Versus Folly

The book of Proverbs spends a whole lot of time making the huge contrast between wisdom and folly, between the wise and the foolish. It paints two such distinct and different portraits: one is blessed by God and leads to blessings in life, while the other is opposed by God and leads to emptiness and destruction. However, they are similar in that they both offer us an invitation to follow, both distinguish themselves clearly, and both boldly proclaim rewards. By getting to know wisdom and folly like the back of your hand, the Holy Spirit will instruct you and God will equip you with the discernment to choose wisdom every time...but the choice is yours. And in essence, our life is broken down into moments whereby we can choose wisdom or we can choose folly. Whatever our decision, be assured that we will eat the fruit of our choice.

Listen to one of my best friends, Bonnie Christensen, CEO of Woman Gone Wise, write about the invitation that wisdom and folly offer each of us every day.

Wisdom has prepared a feast of succulent food and drink. You are invited to pull up a chair and settle in. Listen and join the conversation. You will learn how to 'Leave your simple ways and live, and walk in the way of insight.' Wisdom will openly offer you the foundation for your life, 'The fear of the Lord is the beginning of wisdom, and the knowledge of the Holy One is insight.

The house of folly appears to have a similar invitation. She imitates wisdom's offer. But she (folly) speaks loudly, seductively. She has set herself in a place of influence. She hasn't prepared a feast for you, but suggests you eat from the sweet stolen water and bread eaten secretly. Folly is enticing, risky, and offers immediate pleasure.

The invitation has been sent to you, because you have been trying to walk along a straight and righteous path. Folly endeavors to get you sidetracked. She will prey on your ambition, your flesh and your pride. Sit with folly only for a moment, and she will take advantage of your lack of sense. Little did you know those who have sat in her company have lost their lives; her guests are in the depths of Sheol. [3]

So, let's look more closely at the wise and the foolish. Just to give you an appetizer of what the Word offers us, look up the following verses and fill in how the wise behave and how the foolish act.

	THE WISE	THE FOOLISH
Prov. 13:20		
Prov. 14:1		
Prov. 15:2		
Prov. 27:12		
Prov. 28:26		

Would you start to see each day as a series of opportunities to make wise choices rather than make foolish choices? To view decisions as opportunities to join wisdom rather than partner with folly?

Yes   No   Will pray about it

As a woman pursuing wisdom, remember that God makes the line between the two abundantly clear when He says "*fools despise wisdom*" in Proverbs 1:7. A fool is one who lives like there is no God; and the wise woman lives like there is a God who has called her for a purpose and created her for His glory.

Looking in Your Mirror

Write a prayer to God expressing your new hunger for wisdom or asking God to give you a hunger within your soul.

Choose a verse out of Proverbs 1-4 to memorize that will motivate your heart towards seeking wisdom. Write it out here and share it with your group next week.

What is the biggest challenge or obstacle to you becoming wise--seeking it or choosing it? Why?

In your own words, explain how becoming a wise woman is a clear indication that you have been "marked by God."

*In the future, I encourage you to read through Proverbs one chapter a day. If you choose a month with 31 days, you have a chapter for each day.

*In the future, I also encourage you to begin a journal with two headings: "Wisdom" and "Folly." Read a chapter or a portion of Proverbs each day and record any instruction on wisdom and write it under "Wisdom." Look for any instruction on what is folly or what the foolish person does and record it under "Folly." You will create an amazing resource of Wisdom.

Last Look in the Mirror

 Reflecting on being a wise woman, ask yourself the following:

What stands out to you about God and His character today?

What is the one thing that you learned about yourself today?

How do these answers relate to your present life? What could they be saying to your mind, emotions, or will?

 God has spoken to my heart. What is the one thing I can change/add/ stop or continue growing in?

Let's have a little fun - If you were to get a tattoo illustrating that you have been marked by God's wisdom, what would it look like? (Sketch it here.)

ANSWERS

A bird in the hand is worth two in the bush.

Go to the ant, you sluggard, consider her ways, and be wise.

A fool and his money are soon parted.

Can a man scoop fire into his lap without his clothes being burned?

Actions speak louder than words.

Spare the rod, spoil the child.

Pride goes before destruction, a haughty spirit before a fall.

A man is known by the company he keeps.

A gentle answer turns away wrath, but a harsh word stirs up anger.

A friend in need is a friend indeed.

[1]   "Knowledge." *Merriam-Webster.com*. Merriam-Webster, n.d. Web. 12 Oct. 2013. <http://www.merriam-webster.com/dictionary/knowledge>.

[2]   "Wisdom." *Merriam-Webster.com*. Merriam-Webster, n.d. Web. 12 Oct. 2013. <http://www.merriam-webster.com/dictionary/wisdom>.

[3]   Christensen, Bonnie. "Your Personal Invitation from the House of Wisdom and the House of Folly." *Woman Gone Wise*. Wordpress, 09 Aug. 2011. Web. Web. 16 Jan. 2013.

Leaving His Mark

Marked by Him

I Am A Woman Who Fears Her God

It's hard to lay aside your list for the day or all the things circling in your mind, but now is the time to do that. You can only truly be present in this moment if you engage in this time. Ask God to help you give Him your full attention.

As we continue to look in the mirror, we contemplate the question of what kind of compelling influence do we want to have in this world? We know that our influence comes from who we are; and out of who we are, flows what we do.

Review what you have learned by filling in the blanks from the past two days:
If you've been marked by God Himself, then you are able to say,
I am deeply _____.
I am a _____ woman.

Today if you've been marked by God, then you are able to say, **"I am a woman who fears her God."**

Fearing God

"Charm is deceitful and beauty is vain, but a woman who
fears the Lord, she shall be praised." Prov. 31:30 NASB

Why do you think God mentions charm and beauty as the opposite desire of fearing God?

If 1 John 4:18 teaches us that "There is no fear in love. But perfect love drives out fear...," then why do you think God would tell us we are praiseworthy women if we live in the fear of Him?

Today, we are going to answer that question.

Open the Scriptures to learn what God means by *"the fear of the Lord."* Then look in His mirror to determine whether that fear is true in your heart and life.

Looking in God's Mirror

Fearing God: This is Big Stuff

We are taught in Proverbs 1:7 that *"the fear of the Lord is the beginning of knowledge"* and in Proverbs 9:10 that *"fear of the Lord is the beginning of wisdom."* In other words, the fear of the Lord needs to be the foundation upon which we build our lives. It is the start or the groundwork for our knowledge of Him and how we apply His truth to our living. Fearing God is what gives us the right perspective and what literally prompts or motivates us to use that fear towards the right end. It completely determines your outlook.

I noticed this whole new concept of fearing God in college when I began studying the Old Testament. I kept reading over and over about those who feared God, and how God expected to be feared, and we were blessed if we feared Him. Here, read some of what I was reading and tell me what goes through your mind.

"So that you, your children and their children after them may fear the LORD your God as long as you live by keeping all his decrees and commands that I give you, and so that you may enjoy long life." Deuteronomy 6:2

"And now, Israel, what does the LORD your God ask of you but to fear the LORD your God, to walk in obedience to him, to love him, to serve the LORD your God with all your heart and with all your soul." Deuteronomy 10:12

"He did this so that all the peoples of the earth might know that the hand of the LORD is powerful and so that you might always fear the LORD your God." Joshua 4:24

"But be sure to fear the LORD and serve him faithfully with all your heart; consider what great things he has done for you." 1 Samuel 12:24

"For great is the LORD and most worthy of praise; he is to be feared above all gods." 1 Chronicles 16:25

Then the LORD said to Satan, "Have you considered my servant Job? There is no one on earth like him; he is blameless and upright, a man who fears God and shuns evil." Job 1:8

"The fear of the LORD is pure, enduring forever. The decrees of the LORD are firm, and all of them are righteous." Psalms 19:9

"Whoever fears the LORD has a secure fortress, and for their children it will be a refuge. The fear of the LORD is a fountain of life, turning a person from the snares of death." Proverbs 14:26-27

"The Spirit of the LORD will rest on him--the Spirit of wisdom and of understanding, the Spirit of counsel and of might, the Spirit of the knowledge and fear of the LORD..." Isaiah 11:2

"'Should you not fear me?' declares the LORD. 'Should you not tremble in my presence? I made the sand a boundary for the sea, an everlasting barrier it cannot cross. The waves may roll, but they cannot prevail; they may roar, but they cannot cross it.'" Jeremiah 5:22

What are your thoughts right now about how important or how much God wants you to fear Him?

There are numerous other Scriptures that teach about the fear of the Lord and many of our Bible heroes were described as ones who feared their God. Its first mention is in Genesis 20:11 and its last mention is in Revelation 19:5. It is no small subject, and yet I have heard so little taught about it. So I dedicated a summer to studying what it meant to fear God, meditating on Scripture that grew my Godly fear and journaling my growth and understanding of being a woman who fears the Lord. Similar to any in-depth study of God's Word, my life has never been the same and my outlook has been affected for eternity. I am so excited for you to spend some time today studying this incredible way God marks His people!

Defining This Fear

The common use of the word fear is centered on dread, fright, or apprehension. It is considered a troublesome emotion that perceives someone or something as dangerous, likely to cause pain, or a threat. Thus, we can see why God teaches that His perfect love casts out this kind of fear. Our Heavenly Father doesn't threaten His children with harm; He warns us of consequences. He doesn't place us in peril; we choose to do that by going our own way. He doesn't bring pain to our souls; He came to heal the brokenhearted and will use pain for our growth and His perfect purposes. This common use of "*fear*" might give a glimpse of one aspect of "*the fear of the Lord*," but, by no means, defines what God is talking about when He tells us to fear Him and His name.

Most commentaries will explain "the fear of the Lord" as an all-encompassing, reverential awe of the Most High God. This is a wholesome fear that doesn't spring from dread of one's power, but out of such a high estimate of one's character. Power alone would elicit a hateful, bitter kind of fear. Goodness alone weakens or lessens the reverence. Our Almighty God has them both and so much more--Hallelujah! Knowing God's character becomes crucial to fearing Him.

In light of this definition, I want to unpack what "this all-encompassing, reverential awe of the Most High God" involves by using four key elements. I'm basing these four elements on Jerry Bridge's book (which I highly recommend), *The Joy of Fearing God.* [1]

God's Character That You Need to Know

In Order to Rightly Fear Him - #1 You Need To Know His Greatness [1]

Throughout the Bible the display of God's raw power is recorded in order to develop trust in His people. Who else parted the Red Sea, spoke light into being, shut the mouths of lions, tore open the earth to swallow some rebels, dried up the River Jordan, had a big fish throw up a servant, took down the fortifying walls of Jericho, flooded the entire earth's surface, turned a woman into a pillar of salt, brought a dead child back to life, fed 5000 with a boy's lunch, or turned the world upside down with twelve men? Who?

"Great is the Lord and most worthy of praise; His greatness no one can fathom." (Psalms 145:3) Our God Jehovah has infinite greatness. No one else has or ever will have His power.

Within Isaiah 40:12,15,17, and 23-26, how do you see God's great power?

God is greater than all creation, all nations of this world, and all of the nations' rulers.

Note the immensity of God. (1) We don't know the distance across the universe, but we do know how far away the nearest star is--26,000,000,000,000 miles or 4 1/2 light years away. (2) God says He marked off the heavens by the breadth of His hand, and do you realize that scientists estimate the distance of the universe to be anywhere between 1-14 billion light years away?

"I am the LORD, and there is no other; apart from me there is no God." (Isaiah 45:5) The Lord God's greatness is not only immense, but it is incomparable.

How do you see His incomparable greatness in Jeremiah 32:27 and Matthew 19:26?

Sister, we need to know the greatness of the God of ancient days. His powerful immensity and incomparability should result in our fearing His name.

In Order to Rightly Fear Him - #2 You Need To Know His Holiness[1]

One of my favorite explanations of God's holiness is by a dear brother in Christ who taught me in Sunday school that God's holiness is His complete separateness from mankind, and even His separateness from the spiritual beings. It is much more than His moral purity which many define it as. It is the sum total of all His attributes that equate to divine perfection, and which sets Him totally apart from us.

In Isaiah 6:3 we read, *"Holy, holy, holy is the Lord Almighty; the whole earth is full of His Glory."* The Hebrew language uses repetition to create emphasis, much like we would make a font bold or underlined or all caps. Interestingly, we never find in God's Word any other part of His nature repeated three times--not "kind, kind, kind" or "faithful, faithful, faithful." The writer is calling God's holiness to the highest exaltation.

R.C. Sproul uses the word "transcendence" to describe God's holiness:
"When we speak of the transcendence of God we are talking about that sense in which God is above and beyond us. It tries to get His supreme and altogether greatness...Transcendence describes God in His consuming majesty, His exalted loftiness. It points to the infinite distance that separates Him from every other creature." [2]

This holiness of God calls for a particular response from each of His children--one of utter humility! Echoing Isaiah's deep realization when confronted with the holiness of God, we too can say, *"Woe is me! I am a man/woman of unclean lips"* (Is. 6:5). God has entrusted each of His followers with a stewardship of obedience that we choose to repeatedly rebel against. We defy the ways of our supreme God. We revolt against the holiness of our Lord God. If the revelation of our own heart's treason and God's transcendent majesty doesn't bring about humility, I don't know what will.

Our humility leads to fear as we understand that we are being held accountable for each unconfessed sin, whether in thought, word, or deed. To live without this fear, some might say, is the root of all wickedness. Our society today believes that they are accountable to no one other than themselves. They don't believe there exists One who has the power and the authority to bring them into judgment. In my eyes, you cannot get much scarier than that!

Read Romans 3:10-18 and write out verse 18.

What can you learn from Matthew 12:36-37 and 2 Corinthians 5:10 about your future judgment?

There most definitely is a Judge. His name is Jesus Christ and He has been given the authority to judge from His Father. Knowing that we are held accountable should not only humble us but produce a beautifully deep fear of the Lord.

In Order to Rightly Fear Him - #3 You Need To Know His Wisdom in Design[1]

We can't help but grow in our fear of the Lord by coming to appreciate His incomprehensible wisdom and divine orchestration. His wisdom knows the best means of accomplishing the best end, and the best end is always His glory.

Creation is God's skill and splendor on display, much like an art gallery full of masterpieces. Most incredible engineering feats are done by a team and are perfected through trial and error, yet God needed neither. He alone is the Master Creator and He is the sole Sustainer. *"For from Him and through Him and to Him are all things. To Him be the glory forever! Amen"* (Romans 11:36).

For instance, consider the ingenuity of the heart in our body. "Think what a challenge it would be for a team of engineers to design a pump with these specifications:

75-year life expectancy (2,500,000 cycles)
Requiring no maintenance or lubrication
Output varying between .025 horsepower and
short bursts of one horsepower
Weight not exceeding 10.5 ounces
Capacity of 2,000 gallons per day
Valves operating 4,000-5,000 times per hour" [3]

God's skill is beyond human, finite understanding. However, He doesn't just create; He sustains and cares for all of His creation.

Please be blessed as you read Psalms 104:10-24.

"He Himself gives all men life and breath." (Acts 17:25)

"He ... supplies seed to the sower and bread for food."(2 Corinthians 9:10)

"All things have been created through Him and for Him. He is before all things, and in Him all things hold together." (Colossians1:16b-17)

The overwhelming truth that God sovereignly orchestrates every individual life within the scope of His global master plan is far beyond the finite mind. Yet we can rest in the promise that He *"works all things together for the good of those who love Him, who have been called according to His purpose"* (Romans 8:28). Furthermore, His ultimate plan of redemption is like a scarlet thread woven through history in ways we never would have imagined, against all odds, using the most unlikely people, and within a time frame that only becomes clear in hindsight. However, the beauty and brilliance of His design is like a climactic crashing of cymbals! And know this, His plans cannot be manipulated or stopped.

How do you see God's Divine orchestration in Job 42:2 and Proverbs 16:9?

We are not God's counselor or mentor; who are we to think that the designer of the human body needs help managing our life and circumstances? When we meditate on the wisdom of the Most High that created and directs this world for His glory, we can't help but begin to fear the Lord.

In Order to Rightly Fear Him - #4 You Need To Know His Love [1]

There's something about the love of God that should take your breath away. One of my favorite lines of any hymn is "Amazing love! How can it be? That Thou my God shouldst die for me?"[4] I cannot fathom the depth, the breadth, or the height of His love for me, a sinner. I know who I really am--what I think, what I lust for, what I'm motivated by, what I really want to say and what I do say, what I do--I know it all. And so does God. Yet, He loves me. He loves me so much that His love has turned away His wrath from me. Even beyond that, His love bestows grace on my life.

The Almighty God's wrath is another "not so talked about" topic. It's uncomfortable to realize God is determined to punish sin with a vengeance because we know that we fall under the category of those who sin. Before becoming Christ-followers, Scripture teaches that we were objects of God's wrath, but that the atonement of Christ's death was an act of God's love. His sacrificial love sent Jesus Christ to suffer His wrath, a suffering far worse than the physical torture. When Jesus cried out, *"My God, my God! Why hast Thou forsaken Me"* (Matthew 27:46), He was bearing the wrath of God that was due to you and me! How can that not make us gasp in amazement? Do you understand that God's wrath is what flooded the entire earth's surface in judgment and that which He promises will judge the earth with fire next time (2 Peter 3:10)? This is the wrath that Jesus bore. The future judgment isn't what should cause us to gasp; it's the love that turns His eternal wrath away from our hearts.

Which of these sacrifices that Jesus made translates as the most loving to you? Explain.

Jesus leaving heaven
Jesus taking on humanity
Jesus suffering God's wrath that belonged to you
Jesus suffering the cruelest physical torture
Jesus dying to make a relationship possible with you

If turning away the wrath of God towards each of us isn't enough to overwhelm our hearts, God's love gives us grace upon grace through Jesus Christ. Many say that grace is unmerited favor, a gift which we have not earned. But the truth is that God's grace given to you in love through Jesus is actually far more than that. It's favor being shown to one who not only didn't earn it but deserves judgment, to one who should be punished but instead receives grace. For example, giving a homeless person a meal that he did nothing for is not grace--it's kindness. Grace is knowing that homeless person broke into your car and stole your wallet and iPod, and then giving him/her a meal.

Through Christ's atonement, grace is defined as being given bountiful favor with God instead of the deserved eternal death. (Are you having a hard time catching your breath yet? This truth just takes my breath away.) Every blessing you receive, every answered prayer, every moment of peace, every precious hope, every one of those moments where God touches you in a deep way is grace! And His grace abounds towards us!

Share the last spiritual blessing God favored you with.

Fearing the Lord includes being amazed and astounded by His love for you!

Looking in Your Mirror

Considering the four aspects of fearing God, rate where your heart is at in each area.

I Respect His Greatness
Minimally --- Fully

I Fear His Holiness
Minimally --- Fully

I Admire His Wisdom
Minimally --- Fully

I Am Amazed by His Love
Minimally --- Fully

Which aspect of fearing God do you need to grow in? Circle it.

What can you do to grow deeper in your fear of God?

Spend a moment praying about how strongly/weakly you fear the Lord.

Last Look in the Mirror

Reflecting on what it means to fear God, ask yourself the following:

What stands out to you about God and His character today?

What is the one thing that you learned about yourself today?

How do these answers relate to your present life? What could they be saying to your mind, emotions, or will?

God has spoken to your heart. What is the one thing I can change/add/ stop or continue growing in?

Let's have a little fun - If you were to get a tattoo to show that you have been marked by the fear of God, what would it look like? (Sketch it here.)

Let me pray for all of us.

> *"Almighty God and Creator, we humbly bow before You in utter amazement this day. You alone are Holy. You alone are good. You alone are wise. And You alone are God. You do all things well.*
> *Never let us develop amnesia or become blind to the reality of Who You are and who we are. Convict us when we get confused and think of ourselves more highly than we ought. Stir within each of our souls a deep and abiding fear of Jehovah--one that holds us to sober accountability, kissing your feet in adoration, and forever being blown away by our God!*
> *All for Your Glory. Amen."*

1   Bridges, Jerry. *The Joy of Fearing God*. Colorado Springs, CO: Waterbrook Press, 1997. Print.
2   Sproul, R.C. *The Holiness of God* . Wheaton, IL: Tyndale Publishing, 1985. 55. Print.
3   Brand, Paul, and Philip Yancey. *In His Image*. Grand Rapids, MI: Zondervan, 1984. 13. Print.
4   Wesley, Charles. *And Can It Be*. Psalms and Hymns, 1738. Print.

Leaving His Mark

Marked by Him

I Am A Servant

Selah. Pause and ask God to help you meditate on what a servant really looks like and whether you have been marked by Him.

Looking in the mirror today, we again ask ourselves, "How am I going to impact this world for Jesus?" We know that our influence comes from who we are, and out of who we are, flows what we do.

Review by filling in the blanks from the past three days.
    If you've been marked by God Himself, then you are able to say,
        I am deeply _____.
                I am a _____ woman.
        I am a woman who _____.

If you've been marked by God, the fourth distinction is that you are humbly able to say, "**I am a servant.**"

Christ Jesus makes it clear to the crowds, who want to be popular or follow the latest spiritual fad, that He wants people to consider the high cost of following Him. He makes no apologies as He lays out the requirement, "*If anyone would come after Me, he must deny himself and take up his cross daily and follow Me. For whoever wants to save his life will lose it, but whoever loses his life for Me will save it. What good is it for a man to gain the whole world, and yet lose or forfeit his very self*" (Luke 9:23-25)? It is our choice to die to ourselves, our choice to come under His Lordship, and our choice to accept the ransom He paid for our souls. So He tells us to make that choice thoughtfully with all things considered. For once that decision is made, we no longer belong to ourselves because we have been bought with a price--the precious blood of Jesus. Now we are a servant, His servant, left here to be His hands, His feet, and His heart to this world.

 God's truth is counter-cultural, and today's truth is no exception. Proceed with an open spirit.

Looking in God's Mirror

What Does Being Great Look Like?

When you think of "greatness," who comes to your mind and why?

Jesus called the disciples together and said, "*You know that those who are regarded as rulers of the Gentiles lord it over them, and their high officials exercise authority over them. Not so with you. Instead, whoever wants to become great among you must be your servant, and whoever wants to be first must be slave of all. For even the Son of Man did not come to be served, but to serve, and to give his life as a ransom for many.*" Mark 10:42-45

Name at least 3 things you can learn about being a servant from this passage.

The role of Deity on earth was to serve! That is mind-blowing to me! Our God--Holy One, Most High God, Almighty, Jehovah, Elohim, Jehovah-Jireh, I Am, Alpha and Omega, Creator, Sustainer--came to serve. And have you ever thought about whom He came to serve? He did not come to serve the angels who worship Him or the seraphs who hide their face in His presence, He came to serve mankind. He came to serve those who would reject Him, spit on Him, mock Him, rip open His back, drive nails in His hands and feet, hang Him on a cross, and live like He never existed. He came to be great by serving us and now it's our turn to be great by serving Him by serving others. Humility is greatness. Women marked by God know they are servants, here to serve.

Who comes to your mind when you think of humility? Why?

Servanthood is Available and Active

Servanthood is not about your ability, but about your availability and your action. You need an attitude of willingness paired with a heart that will put feet to your eagerness. Do you have the mind of Christ Jesus and the heart of your Savior? The Bible says in Ephesians 2:20, "*We are God's workmanship, created in Christ Jesus to do good works, which God prepared in advance for us to do.*" God made you to make a difference by creating you to serve, saving you to serve, and gifting you to serve. Let's look in the mirror.

Available = Having the Mind of Christ

Being willing to serve starts in your mind--conforming your mind to the mind of Christ.

> "*Do nothing out of selfish ambition or vain conceit. Rather, in humility value others above yourselves, not looking to your own interests but each of you to the interests of the others. In your relationships with one another, have the same mindset as Christ Jesus: Who, being in very nature God, did not consider equality with God something to be used to his own advantage; rather, he made himself nothing by taking the very nature of a servant, being made in human likeness. And being found in appearance as a man, he humbled himself by becoming obedient to death--even death on a cross!*" Philippians 2:3-8

According to this passage, what does your mind need to conform to? Or what truths do you need to lay hold of? (Name at least 3)

Who do you need to value most?   You   Others

Was Jesus forced to be humble?   Yes   No

How far did Christ's humility take Him? _____

Meditate on this question: How far has your humility taken you?

Humility is rooted in a lowliness of mind. I have always defined humility as knowing who I am and knowing who God is and never getting the two confused. When you know who you are, a sinner saved by grace, and know who God is, your Divine Redeemer who died in your place, it becomes an expression of gratitude to put others before yourself so that they might be drawn to the same Lord. The focus of your mind is not centered on feeling equipped, or prepared, or skilled, or a professional at what God calls you to do. Rather, your mind is targeted on being willing and being available because your faith tells you that He will equip you for whatever He asks you to do. Moses never would have led, Jonah never would have gone to Nineveh, Esther never would have approached the king, Peter never would have gotten out of the boat, and Paul never would have stepped foot in a synagogue if their focal point was on being experienced or proficient. Having Christ's mind means you are always ready to follow, always ready to do the will of God.

Write out John 4:34 in your own words.

Before we go on though, let me highlight a few wrong motives of serving that actually lead to being a doormat:

> "If no one will do it, then I must have to do it."
> "I'll do this because I want you to like me."
> "I don't want to take the chance of being excluded in the future."
> "If I don't do this, then you might reject me."

To clarify, an available servant freely chooses to reach out and meet a need with a motive of humility. A doormat, one whose service is often used and abused, has the wrong motivation--she is available out of guilt, fear, and the need to perform--which all point back to herself. She has lost the focus of

Jesus. Remember that God's servant is available to Him at all times to do what God asks her to do--not available to people at all times to do whatever people might ask her to do.

Define "available to serve" in your own words.

What needs to change for your heart to be more available to serve?

As God's servant, your mind needs to be willing to say, "God, I'm free if You need me right now. I am always accessible for You to use. I am at Your disposal, on deck, up for grabs, hand raised, ready, willing, and able!" As the prophet Isaiah said, *"Here I am Lord, send me"* (Isaiah 6:8).

Active = Having the Heart of Christ

Servanthood is active. You can't be passive and be a servant of the King. Our life needs to be about giving, investing, and contributing. Sir William Osler, a founding professor at John Hopkins Hospital, said, "We are here to add what we can do, not get what we can from life." Our Lord Jesus modeled the heart of a servant by the way He gave to others every day of His life. Read one of His amazing acts of service in John 13:1-17.

Jesus is about to show the full extent of His love as He goes to the Cross and becomes sin, bearing the wrath of God. But at this Passover meal He demonstrates love by washing the feet of His disciples. Most of us will not be called to suffer and die in service for our Lord, but we can give our hearts every day in the way we choose to "wash other's feet."

Think with me on this:

Whose feet did He wash? _____

What was one of His twelve disciples about to do? (v. 2) _____

What would another disciple do in the near future? (Matthew 26:69-75)

What would the rest of the disciples do in the coming days? (Matthew 26:56)

If we are to have Christ's heart, how does that challenge you as a servant?

Is there anything else you can learn from His example in these verses?

We haven't been called to talk about servanthood, take classes on being Christ's bondslave, start serving groups, or even study the life of service. Each of those could be beneficial, but not in comparison to actually putting Christ's heart into action and serving. *"Dear children, let us not love with words or speech but with actions and in truth"* (1John 3:18).

There are many hindrances to being a servant--pride, inconvenience, materialism--to name a few. "Thinking like a servant is difficult because it challenges the basic problem of my life: I am, by nature, selfish. I think most about me. That's why humility is a daily struggle, a lesson I must relearn over and over. The opportunity to be a servant confronts me dozens of times a day, in which I'm given the choice to decide between meeting my needs or the needs of others. Self-denial is the core of servanthood. Jesus has called all true believers to be servants of others. Your servant's heart will reveal your maturity." [1]

Which of these 3 obstacles is your greatest challenge?

"I'm above that."	*"I don't have time!"*	*"It will cost me!"*
(pride)	*(inconvenient)*	*(materialism)*

When it comes to PRIDE, remember this:
- Pride deceives you. (Obadiah 1:3)
- Pride leads to your downfall. (2 Chronicles 26:16)
- Pride brings disgrace, causes quarrels, and leads to destruction. (Proverbs)
- Pride has no room for God. (Psalms 10:4)

When it comes to being INCONVENIENCED, remember this:
- What if Jesus said, "Could we re-schedule?" to the father begging for his dead child's healing?
- What if Jesus said, "Now just isn't a good time for Me," to the blind man who came to see?
- What if Jesus said, "You'll have to get in line," when you told Him that you wanted to follow Him the rest of your life?

When it comes to MATERIALISM, remember this:
- You can't serve God and money. (Mt. 6:24)
- Everything you have has been a gift from God to you, in order to use for His glory.
- Your life is not about what you have. (Lk. 12:15)

Whether it is pride, inconvenience, or materialism, any of these excuses fall exceedingly short in light of Jesus...embarrassingly short. Do you have the heart of Jesus who came not to be served, but to serve and give His life as a ransom for many?

Looking in Your Mirror

Do you feel like you live a life of service putting Christ's heart into action? If not, why don't you serve more?

Give yourself 2 goals for acts of service within the next month.
1.
2.

Share them with one person who will hold you accountable. Who will that be? _____

Last Look in the Mirror

 Reflecting on being His servant, ask yourself the following:

What stands out to you about God and His character today?

What is the one thing that you learned about yourself today?

How do these answers relate to your present life? What could they be saying to your mind, emotions, or will?

God has spoken to your heart. What is the one thing I can change/add/ stop or continue growing in?

Let's have a little fun - you were to get a tattoo declaring you are a servant of God, what would it look like? (Sketch it here.)

1   Warren, Rick. *The Purpose Driven Life*. Grand Rapids, MI: Zondervan, 2003. 258, 266. Print.

Leaving His Mark

Marked by Him

I Am All About Bringing Him Glory

This is what is most important today. This time. This truth. Ask God to begin a fire in your soul for His glory.

Knowing that "what you do flows out of who you are" emphasizes how important it is for who you are to be marked by your amazing God. The more time you spend with Him, the more likely you are able to say ... (review of past 4 days)

I am deeply _____.
I am a _____ woman.
I am a woman who _____.
I am a _____.

Today we look at the last distinction of being marked by God before we move onto leaving His mark. If you've been marked by God then you are able to humbly say, **"I am all about bringing Him glory."**

When many people talk of Christianity, they only talk in terms of decisions or disciplines or even rules, which we know leads us down the road of legalism. It is incredibly sad to me that people don't talk about following Christ in terms of affections or desires or the passions of their heart. Transformation only comes when a heart is changed.

Amazingly, when the heart is passionate about bringing God glory, the disciplines turn into opportunities for drawing closer to God. They become the out-workings of being overwhelmed by the Most High. So, let's see how much your heart has been transformed by your passions towards your God.

Looking in Your Mirror

Passion can be defined as a strong emotion; zeal, eagerness, intensity, fervor, ardor, and fires are its synonyms. It is a powerful word that communicates your heart is dominated by or easily moved towards something/someone.

Name something you were passionate about between the ages of 8-14.

Name something you are easily moved to strong feelings about now.

What have people accused you of being zealous over?

William Penn said, "Passion is a sort of fever in the mind." William Poe was quoted saying, "With me, poetry has been not a purpose, but a passion. And the passions should be held in reverence." George Hegel, while I don't agree with most of his thoughts, challenges us with the truth that "we may affirm absolutely that nothing great in the world has been accomplished without passions being held in reverence."

So, what might be your purpose that goes beyond aspiration to passion? What "fever" burns in your mind? What passion do you want to use to accomplish great things in this world? Share 3-5 possibilities.

Behold your God! *"I saw the Lord seated on a throne, high and exalted, and the train of his robe filled the temple"* (Isaiah 6:1). Enter His temple now and see Him for Who He claims to be.

Looking in God's Mirror

His Passion is Loud and Clear

Interestingly enough, most of the medieval churches taught that God was void of all passion, but nothing could be further from the truth. God is impassioned! So, what is the object of His passion?

What do you think might be God's passion? Each time I have posed this question, the most common response I get is... "Us! He's passionate about His people."

While He loves us with a love that is unfathomable, we are not His passion. God stands supreme at the center of His own affections. Pastor and friend, Michael Hellum reminds us, "God glorifying Himself is not an egotistical need He has, but it is an outflow of His very perfections."

God prizes and delights in His own glory above all things. Now the term "glory of God" is essentially His unveiled magnificence, power, and excellence being radiated or exemplified in some way. It is His purity and fullness of holy majesty. It refers to a glimpse of His infinite beauty and overflowing wealth of all that is good. Truly, the glory of God is beyond any created thing, and any attempt to put into words what God's glory is like will most definitely fall short.

Our being commanded to bring Him glory is in keeping with the very deepest part of who we are--we cannot possibly find fulfillment unless we are doing that. So it is for our benefit that He commands us to bring Him glory. His passion is to display His glory, not because He needs it, but because we do! I love in Isaiah 61 when God talks about sending Jesus to bind the brokenhearted and to set the captives free. He goes on to say that He heals and comforts in order that we might become mighty oaks with a purpose. And what is that purpose? It is "for the display of His splendor!" Sweet sister, as you grow to know your God and take sheer delight in who He is, the overflow of that delight is the constant display of His splendor.

In the same way that Jesus sought to solely bring glory to His Father, so should we as His daughters. Why do we do the things we do? What motivates all of our choices? What is in the forefront of our minds as we make plans? Our passion should be laser focused on bringing God glory.

The most effective way to prove that God declared His passion loudly and clearly is to take a walk through Biblical history and see what His Word teaches. Gleaning the surface by quickly skimming through Genesis through Revelation, you'll see God's passion over and over. (This overview is based on John Piper's work. [1])

As you read these passages, remember that in the Hebrew culture, names were reflections of the character and carried much weight. God's glory and worth are exhibited in His name as well. Essentially, the phrase of doing something "for God's name sake" is the same as doing something for "His glory." In other words, I live my life for God's namesake.

Creation: Read Genesis 1:26-27. God made man in Whose image? _____ Man's dominion over the world and His filling the world is intended to be a display mirroring forth God Himself.

Tower of Babel: In Genesis 11, man desired to use his genius and make a name for himself. God opposed that effort because our dependence upon Him exalts His Name.

The Exodus: We read in Ezekiel 20:5-10 that is was only for the sake of His Name that He brought Israel out of Egypt. God delivered them so His Name would not be profaned among the nations. Israel was set apart to declare to a world that they may know *"that I am God."*

Jesus' Life, Ministry, and Death: How do you see Jesus' passion for God's glory?

In His Life - John 8:29 _____

In His Ministry - John 17:4 _____

In His Death - John 12:27-28 _____

Body of Christ: How do you see the Church's passion for God's glory in 1 Corinthians 10:31?

New Jerusalem: John is talking about the glorified Church in Revelation 21:23, and we see there the consummation of God's passion as His glory literally becomes our source of light!

If God made His passion so incredibly clear, then I can't help but ask myself if my passion should be His passion? And after reading these verses, it's crystal clear to me. But let's also look at a few other reasons His passion should be my passion, as well as your passion.

His Passion Needs to Become My Passion...Because He Commands It

God's passion should become my passion first and foremost because He commanded me to glorify Him. I chose to obey Jesus as my Master and become His servant. And, as His servant, He asks it of me. *"For you have been bought with a price; therefore, glorify God in your body"* (1 Corinthians 6:20). As my Shepherd, He leads me in His glory for His Name's sake (Psalm 23:3). As part of His body, He clearly states His expectations.

What are His expectations in Romans 15:5-6?

As one of His ambassadors on this earth, I am to represent Him to the lost. *"Live such good lives among the pagans that, though they accuse you of doing wrong, they may see your good deeds and glorify God on the day He visits us"* (1 Peter 2:12). And when I represent Him well, others will take notice and God will be glorified.

What are your instructions as children of Jacob in Psalms 22:23?

I could keep going but I'll end with the one that touches my heart the most. Psalms 86:12 -13 illustrates how we give God glory out of what?

Why do you think this would bring God glory?

Because We Were Created For It

God's passion should become my passion, secondly, because I was created for His glory--the way I think, the way I feel, and the way I act culminate in making Him visible. *"Let your light so shine before men that they may see your good deeds and glorify your Father who is in heaven"* (Matthew 5:16). You and I do not have the power to add to the glory of God, but we can go public with His worth.

217

We cannot fulfill our purpose in life without bringing Him glory because our destiny is tied up in it. He has hard-wired each of us as a unique person to impact this world while we are here. He created us and this world to make His glory known. How do you see this in Psalms 19:1-2 and Isaiah 43:7?

We were not created for ourselves but for the purpose of bringing God and His Name glory. And when we come to Christ, we are acknowledging that, up to that point, we had exchanged God's glory for our own or for this world's. Romans 3:23 tells us that we all have fallen short of God's glory, which is why we need to be redeemed to live out His divine purposes for our lives.

Please read the following fable by George Reavis, *The Animal School.*

Once upon a time the animals decided they must do something heroic to meet the problems of a "new world," so they organized a school.

They had adopted an activity curriculum consisting of running, climbing, swimming and flying. To make it easier to administer the curriculum, all the animals took all the subjects.

The duck was excellent in swimming. In fact, better than his instructor. But he made only passing grades in flying and was very poor in running. Since he was slow in running, he had to stay after school and also drop swimming in order to practice running. This was kept up until his webbed feet were badly worn and he was only average in swimming. But average was acceptable in school so nobody worried about that, except the duck.

The rabbit started at the top of the class in running but had a nervous breakdown because of so much makeup work in swimming.

The squirrel was excellent in climbing until he developed frustration in the flying class where his teacher made him start from the ground up instead of the treetop down. He also developed a "charlie horse" from overexertion and then got a C in climbing and D in running.

What do you think the moral of the fable is?

You were created to bring God glory, but many of you have developed badly worn webbed feet because you're putting all your energy into others' areas of purpose instead of what you were created for. Others of you, like the duck, know you're not at all happy, even if others are fine with your choices. Many of you are like the squirrel and feel like you're getting Cs and Ds in life--just barely getting by. Some of you are like the rabbit, and although others are clueless, you are teetering on the verge of a nervous breakdown. I don't say this lightly; I say this to realistically encourage you to look at the possible reality that you aren't living for what you were created for, and to warn you that kind of living will leave you deeply frustrated. (Don't forget that I was on the verge of suicide by living an empty life that I wasn't designed for.)

Sister, the duck was created to fly and swim--the rabbit to run--the squirrel to climb...and YOU were created to bring God glory! You will never find soul satisfaction outside of lifting His Name.

Because It's the Source Of Our Joy

Many of us who came to be reconciled with God at a later age can testify to the emptiness we grew up with, to that God-shaped void in our souls. Nothing satisfied! Some of us tried what this world has to offer...dating, sex, alcohol, drugs, popularity, success, power and the list goes on. But when alone and looking in the mirror, all we felt was the weight of how much these fell short of making us feel whole. They did not satisfy. They did not fill the void.

Blaise Pascal, Catholic philosopher, has said, "There once was in man a true happiness of which now remains to him only the mark and empty trace, which he in vain tries to fill from all his surroundings, seeking from this absent the help he does not obtain in things present. But these are all inadequate because the infinite abyss can only be filled by an infinite and immutable object." That is to say, only by God Himself! As hard as it may sound, you will never find joy outside of God's glory. You may experience happiness, pleasure, accomplishment, excitement, or success--but you won't find joy outside of God's glory. "*Enter into the joy of your Master*" (Matthew 25:23). Jesus says in John after He talks about bringing God glory with the fruitfulness of our lives, "*These things I have spoken to you, that My joy may be in you, and that your joy may be made full. (John 15:11)*"

Luke 6 takes place as Jesus preaches His famous Sermon on the Mount. In the midst of talking about how to live out eternal Kingdom life, what does Jesus say in Luke 6:23? Read Luke 6:20-23 and answer how that applies to God's glory.

May it be known--shout it from the mountain tops and declare this day that our only true joy is found in bringing our God the glory that is due His Name. Exceeding joy is not when I look to my God for silver and gold, but when my heart is transformed so that the Almighty God becomes far more precious than silver or gold or anything this world has to offer!

Looking in Your Mirror Again

On a scale of 1-10, where is your desire to have God and His glory be your consuming desire?

1   2   3   4   5   6   7   8   9   10

Do you get caught up in making decisions and adding disciplines for your spiritual growth or have you focused on changing the affections of your heart? Do you need to do both? Does it matter which comes first?

What will motivate you the most to make God's glory your passion? (Circle one.)

He Commands It
You Are Created For It
He Is The Only Source Of True Joy

Write a prayer asking God for the change of heart you need in order to be passionate about His glory.

Fill in the blank with your full name:
I, _____, have been created for God's glory!

Last Look in the Mirror

Reflecting on being marked by Him, ask yourself the following:

What stands out to you about God and His character today?

What is the one thing that you learned about yourself today?

How do these answers relate to your present life? What could they be saying to your mind, emotions, or will?

 God has spoken to your heart. What is the one thing I can change/add/ stop or continue growing in?

Let's have a little fun - If you were to get a tattoo to illustrate that your life is all about bringing your God glory, what would it look like? (Sketch it here.)

[1]   Piper, John. *Desiring God*. Sisters, OR: Multnomah Publishers, 1986. Print.

WRAP UP TO YOUR FIFTH WEEK OF STUDY

Before you have a chance at impacting others for His glory, you must first be marked by God Himself. So I ask you this week, "Has His love, wisdom, fear, mastership, and glory changed your life? Does your soul have His permanent ink?" God is more concerned about changing you than using you. Using you is a by-product of genuine transformation. Allowing God to have His way and falling deeper in love with Him have got to become clear priorities in our lives.

Beautiful one, walk in the radical change your God has brought to your heart this week, and enjoy the upcoming challenge God lays before His children who desire to live out their faith.

As You Begin Your Last Week of Study

As I am celebrating birthdays in my late 40s, there is one question that keeps coming to the forefront of my mind, "Have I made the kind of impact for Jesus that I want to?"

As my dear friend battles cancer, goes through surgeries, and faces the latest news, I can't help but look at each day in light of eternity. And as I dialogue with my God on my morning runs, I keep asking Him to make my life count for His glory.

Dear sister, whether you have seventeen years or ninety-seven years on this earth, will your life have left His mark on this world? Will your influence have made a difference for His kingdom? I pray so.

Enjoy this week as you allow God to challenge your heart.

INFLUENCE = LEAVING HIS MARK

DAY 26: Leaving His Mark: I Am Walking Intentionally
How purposeful are you about your character? How intentional are you with your encounters?

DAY 27: Leaving His Mark: I Am Walking Uniquely
Are you dreaming God-sized dreams?

DAY 28: Leaving His Mark: I Am Walking Faithfully
How well are you doing with the "dash" you have been given?

DAY 29: Leaving His Mark: I Am Walking With God's Family
Are you living out the "one anothers" of Scripture?

DAY 30: Leaving His Mark: I Am Walking With The Lost
How do you do when you compare your heartbeat with God's heartbeat for this world?

Leaving His Mark

I Am Walking Intentionally

✋ Close the door to your room. Turn off technology. Remove distractions. Give yourself fully to this upcoming dialogue with God.

Okay, we've hammered it home--"**what you do** flows out of **who you are.**" Have you got it? "Who you are" is how you've allowed God to invade and impact your heart and soul. For memory's sake, fill in the following attributes of being marked by the Almighty:

I am deeply _____.

I am a _____ woman.

I am a woman who _____.

I am a _____.

I am all about _____.

As you are being transformed by God into this kind of young woman, you will find yourself with a million opportunities to leave His mark everywhere you go and on everyone you come into contact with. What an exciting way to live...as if you have your own set of the most beautiful permanent markers and your life leaves swishes and swipes and swirlies all over this world. Wow! I love it! I don't want there to ever be a question that I walked this earth and, far more importantly, Who I walked it for.

Arthur Blessitt has marked this world for Jesus in his own unique way. Read his story:

One night during the turbulent '60s, I heard Jesus speak to me. Jesus told me to take the 12-foot wooden cross off the wall of my West Hollywood coffee house and carry the message of the cross to the world's people.

This simple act of obedience started in 1968 as a short walk up and down the Sunset Strip with the cross on my shoulder. I was compelled by God's love to simply share Jesus with everyone who crossed my path and to offer peace to everyone God brought to me. It wasn't long before my walk up and down Sunset Boulevard turned into a marathon walk from Los Angeles to Washington, DC. My walk across America was over, but there was still more walking to do.

This was the beginning of a worldwide adventure on the road with the cross on my shoulder--meeting peasants and presidents, atheists and missionaries, terrorists and tribal leaders--to share the symbol of the cross and the love of Jesus.

This historic and unprecedented walk has taken me through deserts, jungles, cities and islands across all 7 continents, 315 nations, island groups and territories. In all, I have walked over 38,102 miles across the globe, all on foot. [1]

Today we are going to look at what it means to *walk intentionally* to leave His mark. Breaking it down, the "walk" is your integrity of character, and "intentionally" will be the priority you place on being purposeful about your influence.

 There is only one place to go for Truth--for your guiding light, for your perspective, for your strength. Look and see.

Looking in God's Mirror
Your Walk = Your Integrity of Character

Merriam Webster includes three components in the definition of integrity, which give great insight when looking at character: incorruptibility, soundness, completeness. [2] Let's look into these and how they relate to your integrity of character in Christ.

Incorruptible Character

If your character has integrity, then its moral values are virtually incorruptible. You live by your code of ethics. You are not swayed easily or often, in spite of your changing circumstances. And we all know that it's the circumstance that challenges our character. Anyone can be honest and reliable when life is easy and surrounded by support. It's when you find yourself in the midst of skeptics or people you want to be accepted by that your character can waiver. It's when life kicks the air out of your gut, or you are standing on the verge of a decision that Scripture doesn't have an exact verse for, that your integrity can be corrupted. Simply put, an incorruptible character is like the country song by Blake Shelton, "Who are you when I'm not looking?"

Let's go to God's Word and allow it to reflect His truth about our moral character. What do you see in these verses to (a) Avoid/Get rid of? (b) Have as part of your character? Choose two.

Psalms 101:5b   Proverbs 12:22   1 Corinthians 6:18   Ephesians 4:31- 32
Colossians 3:12-13   Hebrews 10:36   1 Peter 1:13-16

AVOID/GET RID OF   PART OF YOUR CHARACTER

What circumstances shake your character the most easily? Cause you to be corrupted?

God gives us two clear ways to protect our character and we would be wise women to act on both. One can be found in the Psalms and the other is taught by Paul in Corinthians.

Key Protection #1

"I have hidden your word in my heart that I might not sin against you." Psalms 119:11

Key Protection #2

"Do not be misled: 'Bad company corrupts good character.'" 1 Corinthians 15:33

Do you think memorizing Scripture and surrounding yourself with the right kind of people protects your character? How so?

O Lord God, please help me keep my character incorruptible. I feel more and more like an alien in this culture...more and more like a salmon swimming upstream while everybody else is cruising downstream...but I long to have a character of integrity. Give me a longing to memorize Your Word and guide me to quality women that can surround and protect me. All for Your glory, Amen.

Sound Character

If your character is sound, it is firm, strong, and free from decay. What gives your character its strength is its consistency. Sound character can be relied upon to be the same regardless of changing circumstances or surroundings. I hear so often from a friend how she is hurting over another's actions and my first question is always, "But is it consistent with who they are?" And the answer is almost always, "yes." People who hurt others are usually consistent in their character. Relational takers are consistently taking. Mean girls are persistently mean. Selfish people think of only themselves. Even though these are the kind of people we don't want to be close to, the point is that they have sound character because it's consistent. You can have a wonderful sound character or a terrible sound character. The question is what does your consistency reveal?

Counselor and friend Myrna Rempel says, "Human nature is that we are creatures of habit. When it comes to character change nothing will change without purposeful work. On average it takes around 66 days of consistent practice for change to feel automatic. Most character is very sound and ingrained in people, which is why when people show you who they really are you need to pay attention. Their character is very sound but not necessarily very good."

Note: Some of you might be wondering what inconsistency reveals...it reveals a lack of character that hasn't developed integrity. Let me clarify that consistent character is not perfect character. As sinners, we are all inconsistent, thus all imperfect. The distinction is between whether we have character that is perpetually inconsistent or all over the map, or whether we are faithfully trying to be consistent.

How would Paul explain consistency in character? 2 Corinthians 8:21

Healthy sound character is free from decay or disease. The dentist has taught us that we need preventative care to keep our teeth and gums free from the attack of tooth decay or gum disease. Ladies, let's not fool ourselves. We need preventative care with our character as well. We cannot neglect our character and expect it to remain sound. In fact, many have lost their character, built over a lifetime, in a few foolish moments. We must guard our character and be on the offense.

What insight can you gain from these verses in regards to how you can keep a strong sound character? Proverbs 4:23, 1 Corinthians 16:13, 1 Peter 5:8

Precious Lord, now I am asking for consistency in my life and character. Living like I'm on a roller coaster or as a chameleon, changing with each circumstance, is a very frustrating and an empty way to live. Give me the desire for great sound character and the discipline to guard it well. For my sake and for Your name, Amen.

Complete Character

If your character is complete, it is undivided and truly pure--it has integrity. When talking about an object of metal that has integrity, it would imply that the metal is not pieced together but is comprised of all the same material. Similarly, as a Christ-follower, your character should be of the purest composition based solely on the Word of God. However, many try to base their character on an eclectic gathering of Scriptural truths and worldly philosophic pieces, resulting in a character that falls short of integrity due to a division of loyalty. New Testament writers warn us over and over against being swayed by false teachers or buying into the empty philosophies of our day. Their words inspire me to teach others that our life and its decisions need to be solely based on the Bible, not on the current culture.

Read Matthew 7:15-16 and Romans 16:17-18. Summarize in your own words.

Your character and my character must be rooted in the Word of God and reflecting His truth to this world, or we will find ourselves being refined by God. To purify gold and silver, the metals are melted by fire in a furnace, and then the impurities (called dross) are removed from the surface of the molten metal. Our Father does the same thing with our character; He uses challenges and trials to bring the impurities (anything contrary to His Word) to the surface in order to be skimmed off.

> *"But He knows the way that I take; when He has tested*
> *me, I will come forth as gold." Job 23:10*

> *"In all this you greatly rejoice, though now for a little while you may*
> *have had to suffer grief in all kinds of trials. These have come so that*
> *the proven genuineness of your faith--of greater worth than gold,*
> *which perishes even though refined by fire--may result in praise,*
> *glory and honor when Jesus Christ is revealed." 1 Peter 1:6-7*

God of Truth, please protect me from false thoughts and teachings that my culture tries to get me to buy into. Reveal lies that I've allowed to creep into my character and that I might be blind to. Give me a hunger to be in Your Word daily that I might continually be more like Your Son Jesus. Amen.

Intentionally = The Priority You Place on Being
Purposeful About Your Influence

You must intentionally make choices to effectively influence this world for Jesus Christ. If you desire to make an impact that makes a difference for His Kingdom, then know that it doesn't just happen accidentally or naturally as life progresses. Every relationship you are a part of and every personal encounter is a Divine appointment for influence. What will you do with it?

Every Relationship

The most challenging place to leave His mark is always within your own home, with your own family, since they live with you 24/7. After all, your family sees who you are at your best and who you are at your worst. Somehow it just seems far easier to co-exist with family members, keeping the conversations light and on the surface. But what if you wanted to make a difference in your family? What would need to change?

Have you ever asked yourself what kind of daughter you want to be? What kind of sister you want to be? Niece? Granddaughter? Cousin? How do you take advantage of living in the same house? When was the last time you shared with a family member what God has been teaching you or a prayer request that's heavy on your heart? How are you influencing your family for Christ's name and glory?

I keep a journal for my children to have a record of my relationship with God. I write in my Bible so they can read about intimate times between Jesus and me. As a family, we have dinner questions to learn more about each other and use each holiday as a celebration time to take our relationships deeper with God and each other. I know it is my responsibility and first ministry to impact my family for the Kingdom. Therefore, I am constantly fighting to find new and creative ways to influence my family for the glory of God.

On a scale of 1-10, how purposeful is your influence
towards your family members?
1   2   3   4   5   6   7   8   9   10

Another challenging place to leave His mark is within our friendships, especially with our girlfriends. We have all heard the term "mean girls" in movies, songs, and real life. Unfortunately, there is far more truth to that expression than we'd like to admit. Girls can be very cruel to one another. Insecurity causes a vicious cycle of girls constantly comparing themselves to one another and acting out in ugly ways from this false sense of competition. How sad! We are on the same team--God's girls. Let's start building one another up and cheering each other on.

So, what about your friendships? Do you pray for your friends? Do you point each one towards God every chance you get? Do you carve time out to be able to listen or encourage or step into their world? Do you share how much you appreciate the good choices they are making? According to the latest headlines and studies, women are lonelier and unhappier and less fulfilled than they have ever been and we are being called to be a little Jesus to each one of them. Another woman's life is not your responsibility, but it is your privilege to leave His Mark on their hearts.

Again, on a scale of 1-10, how purposeful is your
influence towards your friends?
1   2   3   4   5   6   7   8   9   10

Your relationships are in your life for a purpose--for God's purpose--are you being obedient to your Divine responsibility?

Every Encounter

"Be wise in the way you act toward outsiders; make the most of every opportunity. Let your conversation be always full of grace, seasoned with salt, so that you may know how to answer everyone." Colossians 4:5-6

Being purposeful about your influence in every encounter is choosing to live with your eyes wide open and with your internal compass pointing towards the heart of God. This is a far easier choice to make when it fits in with our schedules, isn't it (said the Type A woman)? Erwin McManus, pastor of Mosaic, reminds us that most often Divine appointments will look like inconveniences at the front end. [3] It's important, therefore, that we not only view every encounter, but every interruption, every wrong turn, every inconvenience, every daily routine, and every chance crossing of paths as an opportunity to leave His mark. How do you interact with the elderly neighbor, the crying child in line, the sales clerk, the kid walking down the hall alone, the person sitting next to you, etc.? How do you make the most of the moment in time when your paths intersect?

I know some women who take advantage of every encounter--let me introduce you. My mother-in-law begins every day asking God in prayer for opportunities to be a witness for Him that day. She then makes the most of every opportunity, whether she's getting her hair done or running errands or going to one of her grandkids' basketball games. I find it so easy to get caught up in following my own routine, checking the things off my list, and not noticing who is to my right or my left as I go about my day. What I miss out on!

A dear friend I have lives her life making the most of opportunities because she believes that no one crosses her path by chance. Her eyes anticipate and look for people to influence whether she is at the beach with her kids, jogging in her neighborhood, or volunteering for PTA. You cannot believe her stories about encounters with complete strangers that end up as amazing times of influence. And what a legacy to model for your kids!

How purposeful is your influence towards your daily encounters?
1   2   3   4   5   6   7   8   9   10

Looking in Your Mirror

Incorruptible Character

Are your moral values incorruptible? In other words, do you live out your beliefs 24/7? Explain.

Would you like to begin memorizing Scripture as a guard for your character? Y   N   If so, who could keep you accountable? _____

Are you surrounded with the right people to protect and build your character? Y   N

Do any changes come to mind that you need to make?

Sound Character

What does your consistency reveal? Are you effective or ineffective for God?

When it comes to preventing decay or disease, how are you neglecting your character?

What's your game plan to be on guard?

Complete Character

Choose the top 4 qualities that you want to define you from this list that is compiled from God's Word. Circle the 4.

Adaptability	Appreciation	Caring
Cheerfulness/Optimistic	Committed	Confidence
Contentment	Courage	Decisiveness
Encouraging	Enthusiasm	Excellence
Even-tempered	Fairness	Faith

Forgiveness	Friend-worthy	Honesty
Humility	Initiative	Kindness/Compassion
Leadership	Loving	Loyalty
Obedience	Patient	Peacemaker
Perseverance	Prudence	Resilience
Responsibility	Self-Control	Strength
Teamwork	Thriftiness	Wisdom
Work Habits	Other _____	

Intentionality (Choose One)

Choose one family relationship and determine two purposeful things you can do in the next month to influence them.

1.
2.

Choose one friend and determine two purposeful things you can do in the next month to influence him/her.

1.
2.

Pray each morning for the next week to have opportunities to leave His Mark and then keep your eyes open and be ready to influence.

M_ T_ W_ Th_ F_ S_ Su_

Last Look in the Mirror

Reflecting on walking intentionally to leave His mark, ask yourself the following:

What stands out to you about God and His character today?

What is the one thing that you learned about yourself today?

How do these answers relate to your present life? What could they be saying to your mind, emotions, or will?

What is the one thing I can change/add/stop or continue growing in?

1   Blessitt, Arthur. *The Cross: 38,102 Miles, 38 Years, One Mission.* Colorado Springs: Authentic, 2008. Print.

2   "Integrity." *Merriam-Webster.com.* Merriam-Webster, n.d. Web. 14 Oct. 2013. <http:// www.merriam-webster.com/dictionary/integrity>.

3   McManus, Erwin. *Cahsing Daylight: Seize the Power of Every Moment.* Nashville, TN: Thomas Nelson, 2002. 94. Print.

I Leaving His Mark

I Am Walking Uniquely

✋ *"Be still"* (Psalms 46:10). It takes work to be still. It takes effort to be quiet. It's not always comfortable, but it opens a door to gain more from God than you could imagine. So, be still and ask God to hear His whisper for you today.

"I have a dream that my four little children will one day live in a nation where they will not be judged by the color of their skin, but by the content of their character." Martin Luther King Jr. spoke to over 200,000 civil rights supporters about his dream that day from the steps of the Lincoln Memorial. With his conviction clear in his tone and his passion evident with every word, the people present weren't the only ones inspired--he left His mark on America.

Martin Luther King Jr. isn't the only person with a dream. You have a dream too and, like King's, it's been given to you by your Creator. Are you convinced yet about your need to leave His mark on this world? Are you ready and excited about making a difference for Jesus Christ? If yes, then your next step is this--You need to know how **you** are wired to leave His mark. You need to dig down deep in order to discover (drumroll please...) **your dream** that He's already planted within your soul. Your dream is what makes your influence unique. No one else could ever live out your dream the way you can. So, no pressure, but the world literally needs you to live up to your greatness for His glory!

Looking in Your Mirror

Yes, You Do Have a Dream

Let me try to help you define one or more of your dreams for the future by answering the following questions about yourself.

If you were given a ton of money right now, what would you want to spend it on to make a difference?

What issues/things/matters bring out an instantly passionate (positive or negative) response from you?

Are you drawn to a certain group of people--age, limitations, religion, lifestyle, social status?

What are you good at? What comes easily and you enjoy?

What would you love to be known for after you are gone? What kind of legacy would you want to leave to your kids and grandkids?

Frederic Buechner, American writer and theologian, once said, "The place God calls you to be is the place where your deep gladness and the world's deep hunger meet." [1]

Dream big. Dream giant. Dream outside of your ability. Dream God-sized dreams!

Your Dream is Unique and Important

Although your dream may feel common or normal to you, be assured it's not. Your God-given dream is exclusively yours, separated from all other dreams because only you can live it out. "The world desperately needs you to live up to your greatness!" challenges Erwin McManus. [2]

Your dream has a picture of you on the cover! The table of contents lists the chapters devoted to your strengths, your spiritual gifts, your history, your life experiences, your circle of people, and even your weaknesses--all purposefully designed when you were created to bring God glory. And the conclusion will be determined by what you do with what you have been given.

What might your dream be? List 2-3 possibilities.

 Observe. Pay heed. Welcome. Receive. Discover. Recognize. Listen... listen for His voice.

Looking in God's Mirror

You will find yourself in the Parable of the Talents that Jesus shared in Matthew 25:14-30. You are one of the three servants Christ talks about, and it's important for you to realize which one you are. Read the passage and answer these questions:

Each servant was a steward of the talent(s) he had been given. What does it mean to be a steward?

What did the first 2 servants do with their talents and what was the Master's response?

What two rewards were these servants given beyond the praise?

What did the last servant do with his talent and what was the Master's response?

What seemed to be his motive for doing this?

What were his consequences for not investing his talent?

Which servant are you? _____

Have you in any way "buried" your talents? If so, how?

What is this parable saying to you? What is your responsibility?

Young lady, only you can act on your dream and you have been entrusted to do just that. When you keep it buried, it's only a matter of time before you find yourself living a life out of touch with the very center of your life--your heart, mind, and soul. Your purposelessness and disconnect will rob you of joy and leave a void.

Rick Warren, author of The Purpose Driven Life, instructs you, "If you want your life to have impact, focus it!"[3] Purpose gives meaning to your days. It simplifies decisions you make and directions you take because you can evaluate them in light of your dream. Nothing produces passion more quickly than purpose. Dig deep and discover yours. No one else can live out your dream.

What would you say today if God asked you, "What did you do with all that I gave you?"

Looking in Your Mirror

God wants you to know your dream, to value your dream, and then He expects you to act on it.

What steps are you taking to develop your dream? Or, what could be your first two baby steps?

What women could you seek out in your life to help you grow towards this dream? _____

"Don't die with potential" is one of my new personal mantras. In fact, you can find it sitting on my desk in a small crystal frame. Believe me, there is no shortage of things in life that can cause you to put your dream on hold or bury it altogether, but it's your job to invest in it and see it grow. You just might be amazed by the way "one step forward" leads to a step in another direction which leads to yet another and you find yourself in places doing things with people you never imagined--all to the glory of God.

Listen in on how one step of faith lead to another in the life of Christine Caine, founder of A21 Campaign (Abolishing Injustice in the 21st century):

I will never forget the day when I was waiting for my bags to arrive at the Thessaloniki airport. I happened to glance up at the wall opposite from where I stood. I noticed that there were posters on the wall, and that all of them were full of the faces of women and children. Stamped on the bottom of every single one of these faces was the word "MISSING." I could not take my eyes off these posters, and wondered how so many women and children there were that still remained unfound?

Upon my return home, I gathered our team and we began to collaborate about different ways we could help put an end to the injustice of human trafficking. We conducted extensive research on the issue, and visited organizations and projects that were already on the ground making a difference. The more my team and I learned about the issue, the more we felt compelled to take action.

How could the Church allow human beings, created in the very image of God, to be trafficked and sold like cattle? Why is there not more happening to stop this, and why do most people not even know that human trafficking exists? These are the questions that kept bombarding my mind, and the urgency I felt to take action intensified.

We began the A21 Campaign for "the one", and have since seen "the one" rescued and restored, and then that one reaching out to the next one, who was also enslaved. I believe that we will only continue to see more girls rescued, and that their lives will be a testimony to the truth that God is a redeemer, restorer, and rebuilder of destinies, hopes, and dreams. But it really does all start with the ONE. [4]

Christine's God-sized dream began with the feeling of outrage as she stood waiting for her baggage in a Greece airport terminal. Then she took a step towards research which led her to investigate and dig for a current analysis. That led her to a huge step of praying for the most effective strategy, which, in turn lead to sharing her strategy with others and beginning to put key people with similar passions in place. Lastly, she spearheaded leading this comprehensive campaign into the land of Greece. It now has already spread to the Ukraine and is going global as we speak. This world and these suffering women would be far worse off without a faithful woman taking the next step.

Someone once said, "Avoidance of risk is the greatest risk of all." When we think of the risks that Martin Luther King, Jr. or Christine Caine took, don't lose sight of the critical truth that neither of these two did anything supernatural, but each of them did act on the dream that God wove into their souls. And for that, the world has been impacted!

Now, you go do the same and leave an unmistakable imprint on this world for Jesus Christ!

Last Look in the Mirror

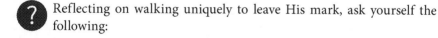 Reflecting on walking uniquely to leave His mark, ask yourself the following:

What stands out to you about God and His character today?

What is the one thing that you learned about yourself today?

How do these answers relate to your present life? What could they be saying to your mind, emotions, or will?

 What is the one thing I can change/add/stop or continue growing in?

1   Buechner, Frederick. "Quotable quotes." *GoodReads*. N.p.. Web. 15 Jan 2014. <http://www.goodreads.com/quotes/140448-the-place-god-calls-you-to-is-the-place-where?page=3>.

2   McManus, Erwin Raphael. Wide Awake. Nashville, TN: Thomas Nelson, 2008. Print.

3   Warren, Rick. *Purpose Driven Life*. Grand Rapids, MI: Zondervan, 2004. Print.

4   Caine, Christine. *Undaunted: Daring to Do What God Calls You to Do*. Grand Rapids, Mich: Zondervan, 2012. Print.

Leaving His Mark

I Am Walking Faithfully

There are sobering questions you need to ask yourself today. There are critical things for you to thoughtfully consider. Ask the Lord to walk alongside of you as you do this.

If God has entrusted you with a dream that is yours alone to act upon, then the next question to ask is whether or not you are faithfully doing just that. Are you investing your talents and your life for the glory of God? Your life is an offering to Almighty Yahweh. It is the incense you burn before His altar of worship, and it is the ultimate gift you lay at His feet.

Think with me for a moment to a time in the future...envision we are at a cemetery and are standing together looking at the headstone at your grave site. Your full name would be engraved on it. There might be a cross, or flower, or some other symbol chosen to adorn it as well. However, the focal point of every grave's granite piece is the dates--imagine your date of birth with a dash and then your date of death. Have you ever thought about the truth that you only have the "dash" to be faithful?

Your "dash" and my "dash" are not very long periods of time in the grand scheme of eternity. In fact, God calls our life a mere vapor (James 4:14). Some are given only 20 years, some might be given closer to 60, and some have over 80 years to make their dash count. But, all would agree that it went far more quickly than they anticipated!

If you could design your own tombstone, what would it look like and what would it say?

Today, you look into the eyes of Jesus and explore whether you are being faithful with the "dash" you have been given.

Looking in God's Mirror

Some might define faithful as any loyal or steadfast following or adhering firmly and devotedly to something or someone. Can you think of any apostle who more fiercely adhered to God's calling on his life than Paul? In his last words to his spiritual son, Timothy, Paul knows he will soon face his own death in the very near future, and he's given thought to the question about his own "dash." He shares how faithfully he has walked with Christ Jesus.

> *"For I am already being poured out like a drink offering,*
> *and the time for my departure is near. I have fought the good*
> *fight, I have finished the race, I have kept the faith."*
> 2 Timothy 4:6-7

Again ask yourself, what do you want your life of influence to say and what kind of impact do you want to have made? With our hearts ablaze for God's glory, each one of us should have these words as the longing cry for our own "dashes":

I have fought the good fight. I have finished the race.
I have kept the faith.

Faithfully: I Have Fought the Good Fight

Every reader in Paul's time would recognize this wording in the context of the Grecian games. The word "fought" is *agonizomai,* meaning to devote serious effort or energy. We get the word "agony" from it, suggesting persistent effort as in contending with an adversary. Paul is painting a picture for an intense struggle for victory.

In the boxing ring, the gloves of the Greek boxer were fur lined inside, but the outside were ox-hide with lead and pieces of iron sewn in. More than the strength of the punch would injure the opponent. The loser of a Greek wrestling match often had his eyes gouged out. Can you imagine the motivation to give your all in these athletic matches? There was no holding back or half-hearted efforts.

Are you willing to intensely struggle for living out your dream? How much are you willing to fight for making a difference for His name's sake? There is an enemy who will battle for your will to give up. He will punch you when you least expect it, and it will probably come from your blind side. He loves to knock you off your feet or lull you into thinking there is no battle going on. Take a look and gain some inspiration from these people who are great successes, yet failed at first: Henry Ford, Bill Gates, Akio Morita (Sony), Walt Disney, Marilyn Monroe, Elvis Presley, Michael Jordan, Emily Dickinson, Abraham Lincoln, Winston Churchill.

Are you facing any attacks or struggles that are keeping you from living out your dream? If so, what are they? Or have you been duped into thinking that you won't be opposed?

Agonizomai is in the perfect tense which indicates a past completed action with ongoing effect. In other words, the moment you were saved the bell rings marking the beginning of "round one" and the struggle persists to the very last round of life. This is a lifelong fight.

Think of a time you needed to follow through with a commitment regardless of the difficulty involved. How well did you do? What were factors in your faithfulness or factors in your quitting? What do you need to learn from that?

So, from this day forward, how will you faithfully fight this fight you have been called to? What do you think will be critical for you to know and to do? Read Revelation 2:10 and 13:10. From these verses, what can you learn about being faithful fighters?

For me, it's most critical to know Who I am fighting for. My dash is fighting for my precious Lord and Savior and for His name to be exalted. That is worth everything I have to give.

Faithfully: I Have Finished the Race

Fellow runner, we don't just have one shot at this dash--one shot at this race. We only have one shot at finishing! And, we are judged by what we finish, not by what we start. The word "finished" used in this verse is *teleo*, which is also used in the perfect tense emphasizing the permanence of the finish. Paul is saying the finish line has been crossed in his life and the results would last forever.

I trained for a marathon a few years back because it was on my bucket list. The truth was that it didn't matter how I started the race that morning in Sacramento, California--what mattered was that I crossed the finish line. Only then did I get the foil blanket to warm my body. Only then did I receive the marathon medal and finisher shirt. Only then did I receive my official time and ranking. And, only then, did I realize that I felt far more accomplishment than I could have ever imagined! I can't imagine the thrills and chills of crossing my finish line into eternity!

As you contemplate how you will finish, I want to remind you that your race to finish has its own course designed just for you. Each of us has been called to a different course, and please don't waste your time or energy comparing your course to everybody else's. You have been given everything you need to run your race--your strengths, your weaknesses, your life experiences, your gifting, your history, your future, and the power of your Holy Spirit.

What can you glean from these passages about your equipping for the race that has been laid out before you? Psalms 18:31-36, 2 Timothy 3:16-17

As we run our race, you and I need to keep asking ourselves: "Am I running well? Am I running faithfully?" I long to cross that finish line running into Jesus's arms and having Him whisper in my ear or yell for all to hear, "Well done my good and faithful daughter!"

According to Hebrews12:1, what do we need to do in order to run well and finish our race?

Races actually have drop off places along the course to shed gloves, hats, water bottles, jackets, and extra layers--anything that impedes you.

What unnecessary weight is hindering you from your race? What sin is tripping you up?

Spend time confessing those before God and expressing your desire to run freely.

Please don't forget that you have your very own cheering section in the heavens who are screaming like crazy for you and your race. Can you just imagine Moses yelling with his staff held high or Peter giving out a loud "Wahoo!" They have not only finished their race, but they have their own cheering section just for your "dash!"

We need to heed the words of the track coach who said, "If you have anything left ten yards past the finish line, you didn't give your all."

Faithfully: I Have Kept Faith

Can you visualize Paul standing before God declaring, "the faith committed to my care, I like a soldier have kept safely through everlasting vigilance, and have delivered it again to my only Captain" (based on 2 Timothy 4:6-7)? I can. The word "kept" is *tereo*, which carries the idea to protect as the result of guarding. Each of us has been entrusted with faith in the Good News that we, too, need to watch guard over. As we influence those around us, our influence must be grounded in the truth of the Gospel itself.

It is evident in all of Paul's letters that he kept his eye on the faith message, carefully watching for those who would try to add to or subtract from the salvation message. Paul contended earnestly for the integrity of the faith as the writer of Jude tells us to do in Jude 1:3-4.

How are you at guarding your faith? Are you constantly checking for the integrity of what you are listening to, reading, or studying?

Do you stand as a soldier publicly when you hear lies, deception, or empty philosophy? Remember that silence is agreement.

In Paul's final hours, what was his clear charge to his young disciple Timothy? 1 Timothy 6:20, 2 Timothy 1:13-14

As a young woman of influence, the one message that needs to be crystal clear in your heart and mind is the message of salvation. Many know they believe but few know what they believe. Let's see how well you know what you have placed your faith in.

Write 1-2 sentences about the following:

Who is God the Father?

Who is Jesus Christ the Son?

Who is the Holy Spirit?

How Are You Saved?

My dear sister, we too have been charged to guard the faith, the glorious treasure of the Gospel. In the midst of this hostile culture, never forget that the Gospel is the only message that can impact heaven with one more saved soul.

Looking in Your Mirror

How well are you doing with the "dash" you have been given so far?

Write your own life's mission statement. It can only be one sentence in length that encapsulates your purpose for your entire life. It could be what you'd name your race course or what you would love to see engraved on your tombstone. (Examples--"Glorify God by giving 100% to all I do," "Only God and people count," "Trust and obey")

Walking faithfully--that means you don't give up. You keep on going. You don't give in. You don't quit halfway through. You don't stop when it gets harder than you imagined. You hang tough and you are able to say "it is finished" at the end of your dash.

And God will say, *"Well done good and faithful servant! You have been faithful with a few things so; I will put you in charge of many things. Come and share your master's happiness"* (Matthew 25:21).

Last Look in the Mirror

 Reflecting on walking faithfully to leave His mark, ask yourself the following:

What stands out to you about God and His character today?

What is the one thing that you learned about yourself today?

How do these answers relate to your present life? What could they be saying to your mind, emotions, or will?

What is the one thing I can change/add/stop or continue growing in?

I just received an email this morning about an incredibly faithful brother, Leo O'Conner. He is younger than me and has just entered hospice care. Leo is a devoted husband with two precious little boys under the age of 10, and we have all been fervently praying for his healing.

My husband and I met Leo and his family a few years ago when he came to the community group we lead and shared his testimony. As he told his story of a bold, deep faith that had pioneered fruitful ministries in South Africa, God and Leo impacted each of us in that room. Our vision of God grew bigger and Leo's example convicted our comfortable evangelism.

Ever since that night, we have been conspiring with Leo to bring our family to South Africa to come alongside and serve with him in his various ministry efforts.

However, at this point in time, God seems to be choosing to bring our brother home to heal him completely. If Leo has the privilege of speaking to Jesus tomorrow, he will be a man who hears his Redeeming Lord say, "Well done, my good and faithful servant. Enter into the joy of your Master!"

Make no mistake, Leo O'Connor has made an impact with his "dash."

Holy Master and Abba, may I be faithful with this "dash" you have entrusted to me. I long to hear Your voice say, "Well done, precious daughter."

Leaving His Mark

I Am Walking With God's Family

Shhhh! It's time to hush the noises of the outside world and invite the quiet into this time with God. Call on God to lead the way today and to have His way in your heart.

Every human being is born with three basic psychological needs: the need for value, the need for competence, and the need for belonging. It's amazing to me that as our world of technology grows at the speed of light, our world of isolation and loneliness seems to parallel it. Never before have women been lonelier. Women are desperate to have their needs met and I am blown away (what's new?) by God's incredible design to meet all three within the community of believers. Simply put, your need for value is met within the sacrificial death of a God who sent His Son to die for your sin. Your need to feel competent is met at the time of salvation when the Holy Spirit entrusts you with your own spiritual gift(s). And your need for belonging is met at that same moment when your name is written in the Book of Life and you become part of the family of God, never to be plucked from His hand. Not only is the family of God designed to be a place where your needs are met at a deep level, but it's created to be a critically important place where you leave His mark.

How are you using your power of influence within the body of Christ right now? How are you leaving His mark?

Bring who you are at this moment and hold it up to the examples in the Bible. Where are you doing well? How do you need to grow? Be prepared to answer these in light of truth.

Looking in God's Mirror
Leaving His Mark Through Prayer

Paul left a strong role model to follow when it comes to praying for your brothers and sisters within the Church. It's evident through his letters that he strongly believed in the power of prayer and the way it wove brotherhood into his life. Perhaps, if you are missing that strong feeling of sisterhood, you need to be praying more for your own? I've always said that nothing knits our hearts together like prayer.

Using Paul as an example, what are specific petitions we can make for our fellow believers? Ephesians 1:18, Philippians 1:9-10, Colossians 1:9

How do you see prayer as an instrument for influence? For leaving His mark?

How is prayer an expression of loving one another? List 5-10 people in the family of God you could start praying for on a consistent basis. How will you keep to that?

Leaving His Mark Through Bearing and Forgiving

"Bear with each other and forgive whatever grievances you may have against one another. Forgive as the Lord forgave you."
Colossians 3:12-13

Bearing with one another is a wonderfully gracious picture. The Greek word for "bear" is in the present tense meaning we continually practice endurance with one another and constantly make allowances for each other.

Guaranteed--people have their own idiosyncrasies. Guaranteed--people will have different perspectives. Guaranteed--people will always let you down. And guaranteed--people will always hurt you.

So, we are being called by God to extend latitude in order to leave His mark on His community of followers. That is not an easy calling, but it is one that leaves a deep impression. Think back to the impression that the Amish community left on the world when they extended forgiveness for what would seem "the impossible."

On October 2, 2006, a gunman entered a one-room Amish school in Nickel Mines, Pennsylvania. In front of twenty-five horrified pupils, Charles Roberts ordered the boys and the teacher to leave. After tying the legs of the ten remaining girls, Roberts prepared to shoot them execution style with an automatic rifle and four hundred rounds of ammunition that he brought for the task. The oldest hostage, a thirteen-year-old, begged Roberts to "shoot me first and let the little ones go." Refusing her offer, he opened fire on all of them, killing five and leaving the others critically wounded. He then shot himself as police stormed the building. His motivation? "I'm angry at God for taking my little daughter," he told the children before the massacre.

The blood was barely dry on the schoolhouse floor when Amish parents brought words of forgiveness to the family of the one who had slain their children.

The outside world was incredulous that such forgiveness could be offered so quickly for such a heinous crime. Of the hundreds of media queries that the authors received about the shooting, questions about forgiveness rose to the top. Forgiveness, in fact, eclipsed the tragic story, trumping the violence and arresting the world's attention.

Three weeks after the shooting, "Amish forgiveness" had appeared in 2,900 news stories worldwide and on 534,000 web sites.

Fresh from the funerals where they had buried their own children, grieving Amish families accounted for half of the seventy-five people who attended the killer's burial. Roberts' widow was deeply moved by their presence as Amish families greeted her and her three children. The forgiveness went beyond talk and graveside presence: the Amish also supported a fund for the shooter's family. [1]

While we cannot imagine what the shooter's wife or family felt like receiving this Scriptural "bearing" and "forgiving," we undoubtedly have been shown latitude many times in our lives that we felt unworthy of receiving.

When have you been at the receiving end of someone cutting you some slack? How did it make you feel?

Who is God bringing to mind right now that you need to show latitude to? (These are the hard people to love, sometimes to even like.) _____

The only thing that can produce a spirit of latitude in our hearts for others is the love of Jesus Christ in and through us. We need to be reminded that we have never been called or appointed to remake others! God is in charge of change and I am in charge of trying, with the Holy Spirit's help, to deal with me and to love God and others well.

Write out your prayer asking God to help you learn how to bear with those in the family of believers you find it especially hard to show the love of Christ to.

I don't know if there is a greater gift of grace we can give to each other than to forgive, yet it can be the hardest one to give depending upon the depth of the hurt inflicted, how many times the offense occurred, or who caused the pain. Our only alternative, however, is to hold onto our grievance, replay it over and over in our head, and eventually become resentful or bitter. Bitterness is one of the cruelest self-inflicting poisons to drink. Not only does it slowly kill us, but it squelches all chance of spiritual growth in and around us. So, in reality, granting forgiveness is our ticket to our own freedom and health.

It's important to also realize a few things that forgiveness is not: It is not dismissing the pain or pretending it didn't hurt. It is not acting like nothing happened. It is not erasing the past. It is not conceding that the offender got away with it. Myrna Rempel wrote in an email to me, "It is not saying it is okay and it is certainly not saying the offender now has to become my best friend. The very fact that we are choosing to forgive...not forget...means a wrong has been done. But you, dear friend, deserve to be free from the emotional entanglement of the person who hurt you. Why did Jesus tell people to go the second mile in Matthew 5 when going the first mile already seemed unfair? The first mile, unfair as it was, was Roman law. Jesus telling people to go the second mile was not cruel, but freedom. The first mile was under Roman control, the second mile was their freedom and their choice. Jesus was empowering people. To not forgive is like that first mile...you are under their control. Forgiveness...is like that second mile...hard and moments that feel like we can't do it, but oh the freedom and renewed strength it gives."

How do we forgive?

> *"Forgive as quickly and completely as the master*
> *forgave you."* Colossians 3:13 (MSG)

So we need to forgive one another as the Master did--**quickly** and **completely**.

Why do you think God wants us to forgive quickly? Do you think He wants us to just skim over the offense or could it possibly be for our own protection? If so, how?

How does forgiving quickly keep someone else, or sin itself, from having power over you?

When I think in light of how I have been forgiven by my Master, I have no right to hold onto anything against another. I am completely undeserving of the forgiveness shown to me over and over again.

If you have forgiven another completely, you have processed the hurt completely. In order to determine whether you have done this or not, use the following as a checklist:

   ___ You are able to say who you are forgiving and what specifically you are forgiving them for. It's very healthy for you to determine exactly what it was that caused you the pain and why!

   ___ You can admit that it was wrong/caused pain--the offender might deny it, but with complete forgiveness you don't trivialize or try to soften the wrongdoing.

   ___ You have no expectations of this person trying to make up for what they did. If they do, great--but you are not expecting it.

   ___ You will not define the offender by the hurt they caused or manipulate them with it. Yowsa--this is hard! This reveals that you are not still hanging onto the offense or using it to prove your case against their character.

___ You do not need to instantly trust this person. It is the offender's responsibility to build trust within the relationship and you recognize that.

___ You choose to continue to grow regardless.

Leaving His Mark Through Encouragement

The word encouragement is used over 100 times in the New Testament revealing its importance to the body of Christ, and I love the image it reveals... to come alongside to strengthen. I know that this lady needs a whole lot of encouragement in her life, and I don't think I'm alone. Nothing beats someone believing in you, cheering you on, lifting you up with their words, a comforting hug, or a reminder of love. It reminds me of the Canadian geese that fly in a v-shaped formation so that the front goose, who takes the lead actually takes the most wind resistance, allowing all the other geese to fly easier. In return, they literally honk encouragement to the goose on point. When I'm out running and I hear them overhead, I imagine them honking, "Keep it up! You can do it! Way to go! You've got this!" It makes me smile. If the geese know to give encouragement to each other as part of the flock, how much more should we be coming alongside of our brothers and sisters in Christ and "honking" really loud?

Let's Encourage One Another With His Word

What is one of the many things God's Word provides us with? Romans 15:4

How are you encouraging one another with God's Word? How could you be?

Nothing sustains us, brings life, anchors our soul, shows us the way, or strengthens us like the living Word of God--nothing! We need to strengthen each other with His promises, His words of comfort, and His commands.

Let's Encourage One Another With Our Words

What does Proverbs 12:18 and 18:21 teach you about the power of words?

Knowing how potentially powerful words can be, let's use them to make a difference in others' lives. Do our words constantly point others towards God? Do our words make others feel supported or loved? Do our words bring refreshment to the weary and comfort, like a warm blanket, to the hurting?

How have you made another stronger with your words? How could you?

Have you ever shared some of your own pain with another in order to let them know they are not alone in their emotions? How so? Read 2 Corinthians1:3-5 and share what stands out to you.

When was the last time you told someone you believed in them? Who was it and what kind of impact did it have?

People need to know they are believed in. There are countless amazing testimonies of what others have accomplished because they felt supported and like someone believed in them. Our history books are full of these stories: Albert Einstein was four years old before he could speak and seven years old before he could read, but he had grandparents who believed in him. Isaac Newton did poorly in grade school, but he had a math teacher who saw something in him and cheered him on. Walt Disney was fired by a newspaper editor because "he had no good ideas," but a doctor thought otherwise and hired him to draw for him. Leo Tolstoy, famous writer, flunked out of college, but a publisher never stopped believing in him. [2]

As women and sisters in Christ, we need to use the power of our words to build beautiful things into each other's hearts and lives. Let's become each other's greatest cheerleaders!

Leaving His Mark by Living Out the "One Anothers"

Our New Testament is full of ways to impact the body of Christ through putting the "one anothers" of Scripture into practice. As I list a few more for your consideration, we cannot miss the crucial element that they all share. We cannot do any of these in our own strength or power. Each one requires the supernatural ability of the Holy Spirit living within. Ask Him to empower you to leave God's mark on the Church by intentionally putting flesh to the "one anothers."

1. John 13:34--"A new commandment I give to you, that you love one another, even as I have loved you, that you also love one another."
2. Romans 12:16--"Be of the same mind toward one another; do not be haughty in mind, but associate with the lowly. Do not be wise in your own estimation."
3. Romans 14:19--"So then we pursue the things which make for peace and the building up of one another."
4. Romans 15:7--"Therefore, accept one another, just as Christ also accepted us to the glory of God."
5. Galatians 5:13--"For you were called to freedom, brethren; only do not turn your freedom into an opportunity for the flesh, but through love serve one another."
6. Galatians 6:2--"Bear one another's burdens, and thereby fulfill the law of Christ."
7. Ephesians 4:25--"Therefore, laying aside falsehood, speak truth each one of you with his neighbor, for we are members of one another."
8. Ephesians 4:32--"Be kind to one another, tender-hearted, forgiving each other, just as God in Christ also has forgiven you."
9. Ephesians 5:21--"... and be subject to one another in the fear of Christ."
10. 1 Thessalonians 4:18--"Therefore comfort one another with these words."
11. Hebrews 3:13--"But encourage one another day after day, as long as it is still called 'Today,' so that none of you will be hardened by the deceitfulness of sin."
12. Hebrews 10:24--"... and let us consider how to stimulate one another to love and good deeds,"
13. James 5:16--"Therefore, confess your sins to one another, and pray for one another so that you may be healed. The effective prayer of a righteous man can accomplish much."
14. 1 Peter 4:9--"Be hospitable to one another without complaint."

Last Look in the Mirror

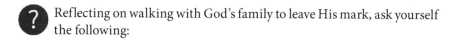 Reflecting on walking with God's family to leave His mark, ask yourself the following:

What stands out to you about God and His character today?

What is the one thing that you learned about yourself today?

How do these answers relate to your present life? What could they be saying to your mind, emotions, or will?

 What is the one thing I can change/add/stop or continue growing in?

---

[1]   Kraybill, Donald B., Steven M. Nolt, and David L. Wever-Zercher. *Amish Grace: How Forgiveness Transcended Tragedy*. New York City, NY: John Wiley & Sons, 2010. Print.

[2]   Unknown, . "Failure List of the Famous." *MotivateUs.com*. Motivating Moments LLC. Web. 16 Jan 2014. <http://www.motivateus.com/stories/famous-failures.htm>.

Leaving His Mark

I Am Walking With The Lost

I truly hope you have begun to develop the practice of stopping life, or stepping away from the noise of your culture each day, to meet with Almighty God Himself. How I pray you have felt the difference of pausing to pray and quieting your soul before you begin. Take the time to do so again.

When we first began this section on influence, we talked about getting marked by God Himself because all we do flows out of who we are, and we want to be women of powerful influence. Words like "deeply in love," "wise," "God-fearing," "servant," and "passionate about His glory" should be descriptive of our character. Then we looked at leaving His mark intentionally, uniquely, and faithfully in our circle of impact, and especially in the family of God.

I am going to get straight to the point today--if we want to leave His mark on this world and the lost, then we need to ask ourselves some pretty straight up questions.

Have you caught on to the practice of looking into His Word for everything? Not opening your spiritual academic book to study, but bringing your heart, your issues, your joys, and your frustrations to His truth and looking for what it is He reveals to you so that you might obey.

Looking in God's Mirror
Two Questions to Ask Your Heart Today:
#1 "Can I Love God & Not Love the Lost?"

In order to answer this question, let's compare our hearts to the heart of God when it comes to the lost souls of this world.

God's Heart is a Seeking Heart;
My Heart Should be a Seeking Heart

How do you see God's heart in action in Luke 19:10?

Please note that God's heart is actively reaching out. He doesn't simply wait for those who are lost to find Him; He initiates and relentlessly pursues each lost soul. His love is not a passive love, a quiet love, or an invisible love. His pursuit should make you feel especially loved. As young women, we know the difference between chasing a guy in hopes that our affection will be returned and being chased by a guy who makes his attraction known. There's not even a question of which "chase" makes us feel more cared about. Please know that the Prince of Peace and Lord of Lords will not remain idle when it comes to your salvation.

How did God seek you out? OR How is God pursuing you now?

How refreshing to know that in His countless pursuits our God doesn't discriminate. His seeking heart is for all. His love is for all. His gospel is for all. His salvation is for all.

What touches your heart about the truths found in 1Timothy 2:1-6?

Are you willing to pray for all?	Yes	No	Not Sure
Are you willing to tell all?	Yes	No	Not Sure
Are you willing to go to all?	Yes	No	Not Sure

God's Heart Rejoices Over a Heart That Repents; My Heart Should Rejoice Over a Heart That Repents

Read Luke 15: Parables of the Lost Sheep, the Lost Coin, and the Lost Son.

What causes the rejoicing in each parable? _____

Share one lesson that you can learn from the Lost Sheep.

Share one lesson that you can learn from the Lost Coin.

Share one lesson that you can learn from the Lost Son.

Who is the last person's repentance you got to rejoice over? _____

What happens if the lost are not found? Revelation 20:11-15, 21:8

You would be hard pressed to find more sobering verses than those that teach us about Hell and the reality of its eternal state. In fact, the most memorable sermon I have heard preached was over 20 years ago by Dr. David Dunn on Hell. And one of the quotes written in my Bible that convicts me the most is that "to have the heart of God is to never grow accustomed to the thud of Christless feet on the pathway to Hell." How can my heart not rejoice over the amazing grace that plucks a soul out of Hell and places them into God's eternal family? And how can I not want to be part of that process?

Pray along with me. *Gracious, loving, merciful, and active God, please don't allow my heart to ever grow accustomed to the lost marching into eternity without You! Amen.*

God's desire for all to come to repentance is most clearly seen in the sacrifice of His Son Jesus Christ as a ransom for all. He longs for every name to be written in the Book of Life. His patience testifies to His desire.

"The Lord is not slow in keeping His promise, as some understand
slowness. Instead He is patient with you, not wanting anyone
to perish, but everyone to come to repentance."
2 Pet. 3:9

Two Questions To Ask Your Heart Today:
#2 "Where Is My Heart For The Poor, The Needy, The Orphan, & The Widow?"

Again, let's compare our heart to the heart of God.

What has He specifically expressed about the poor, the needy, the orphan, and the widow? Proverbs 31:8-9, Luke 12:33, James 1:27

I hear God asking me to have a lifestyle that includes those in different circumstances than my own, and to be ever mindful of the vulnerable. When I live my life being the hands and feet of Jesus to those in need, I am more eternal-minded and authentic in my humility. Truly, life is kept in perspective.

According to Scripture, why shouldn't we neglect the poor, the needy, the orphan, and the widow? Exodus 22:21-27, I John 3:17-18

In Isaiah 10:1-2 God shouts "Woe" as a warning to those who would place themselves on the opposing side of God's heart by not demonstrating compassion for the vulnerable and the victims of injustice. Scripture refers to the poor and the vulnerable hundreds of times from Exodus to Revelation. The concept is so constant that it's virtually impossible to remember God and forget the needy. It strikes me as a display of arrogance and entitlement to somehow think that we are above them. Let's not place ourselves on the wrong side of God's heart.

Let's look at the blessings for those who serve the poor, the needy, the orphan, and the widow. What are the blessings? Proverbs 19:17, Luke 14:12-14

God blesses the compassionate heart that is moved to action on His behalf. It is the fruit of His Spirit to show kindness and a reflection of His heart to love justice. May what was said of Job be able to be said of us!

(Fill in each blank with your name)

> *Whoever heard _____ spoke well of_____,*
> *and those who saw _____ commended _____,*
> *because _____ rescued the poor who cried for help,*
> *and the fatherless who had none to assist them.*
> *The one who was dying blessed _____;*
> *_____ made the widow's heart sing.*
> *_____ put on righteousness as my clothing;*
> *justice was _____'s robe and _____'s turban.*
> *_____ was eyes to the blind and feet to the lame.*
> *_____ was a father to the needy;*
> *_____ took up the case of the stranger.*
> *_____ broke the fangs of the wicked*
> *and snatched the victims from their teeth.*
> Job 29:11-17

Looking in My Mirror

What are My Excuses or Fears?

Do you have any excuses/fears for not sharing the gospel of Christ with the lost? If so, what are they?

Do you have any excuses/fears for not somehow caring for the poor, the needy, the orphan, and the widow?

List each excuse or fear and then determine what each one implies. (For example, Fear of Rejection = It is more important to please man than to please God)

Sweet sister, I am overwhelmed too. Leaving His mark on the lost feels like a daunting task. Am I being asked to live on the streets and care for the homeless or travel the world and serve like Mother Theresa? God, what do you really want from me? What difference can one person really make? In the midst of all those questions, I want us to remember that we are called to influence the circle of people that God has placed us in at this moment in our lives. And when our circle changes, then we influence the new ones in our world. But we are always mindful of the vulnerable and the lost within our circle. And if our circle doesn't include either of those, then we must enlarge our circle.

God is calling out the Hero that lives inside of you--His Holy Spirit. His Spirit wants to reveal Himself to you and to others around you in powerful ways, ways bigger than you can conceive. Never forget Jesus invested His life in twelve ordinary men who were never ordinary again after encountering the Holy Spirit. Neither was the world!

Living Out Loud

It's not enough to know these things, nor is it enough to study these truths. As Steven Curtis Chapman sang in his lyrics, "We need to live out loud!"

In other words, we need to walk our talk. Our actions need to prove our beliefs. Jesus calls us the *"salt of the earth"* and *"the light of the world."* We are here to make a difference. Otherwise, He would have brought us home the moment after salvation. Instead, we are here to tell others the Good News of what Jesus Christ has done for us. And we are here to be the hands and feet of Jesus to the vulnerable and the needy.

My sister, let's put feet to our faith and, in so doing, may our lives literally scream "Jesus!"

Ask God to reveal what needs to be "louder" in your life and where your faith has no action. Confess it and request a new longing to be a different kind of influencer for His glory.

Last Look in the Mirror

God didn't reveal truth to you for the sake of revealing, but for the purpose of building trust, drawing you closer, and exposing both His heart and your heart. Have you developed this practice yet? Always keep asking yourself the needed questions.

What stands out to you about God and His character today?

What is the one thing that you learned about yourself today?

How do these answers relate to your present life? What could they be saying to your mind, emotions, or will?

♥ God seeks response. He desires to transform. Do you believe? Prove it. Never skip the last habitual component of "What needs to change in me?"

What is the one thing I can change/add/stop or continue growing in?

I wish I could hear what you are thinking right now. Are you as challenged as I am? Do you get excited by all the new, crazy ideas that start popping into your mind of how you could reach out, or love, or make a change? Then do you get scared and think, "Who do I think I am?" But if you stop and listen, you can hear God tell your soul, "It's not about you. It's about Me...and I can do anything, anytime, anywhere, and with anyone!"

So, what does God want you to do with your dash? I know one thing for absolute certain...He wants it to be God-sized!

Last Day Together

Live What You've Seen Reflected in the Mirror

As you think back over all the truth that God has taught you in the past weeks, I pray that it will inspire you to continue growing in your faith. There have been numerous truths that will change your life if you just choose to act on them. God has faithfully revealed so much to you, and now it's your turn to put it into action. Let me leave you with some opportunities to do just that. Choose one course of "change" from each section.

<u>To Live Out Your Confidence</u>

Wear your awareness (of yourself & of God) - Confidence is beautiful.

1) Go back to Day 4 and choose one of the goals you set for yourself. Now break it down into 3-5 smaller goals in order to accomplish. Write these smaller goals on your mirror one at a time until completed. Throw a mini-celebration once all are done and your main goal is now a living reality.
2) Choose one of God's character traits and do your own research and study on it for two weeks. Journal all that you learn and discover.

3) Which of the following is hardest for you to believe? You aren't home ~ You are His bride ~ You are His Masterpiece ~ You are justified ~ You are a daughter of the King. Upon choosing one, memorize 2-3 verses from that study so that the Holy Spirit can use them to minister to your heart.

To Live Out Your Freedom

Freedom is worth fighting for!

1) Which area do you still need freedom from--baggage, self-righteousness, fears, worry, strongholds? Re-do that study. Create your own battle plan based on God's directives to rid yourself of its destruction.
2) Find an old key and make your own necklace reminding you that you need to hand over your driving key each day to the Holy Spirit so He can be in charge. Wear it for 2-3 weeks--each time you notice you have it on, give your will and your desires over to the control of His Spirit.
3) Choose one of the Fruits of the Spirit to focus on in your life. Study it. Memorize 2 verses about it. Set your own goals in regards to displaying that fruit.

To Live Out Your Influence

Leaving His Mark

1) When you think of being marked by God, which descriptive is not describing you in the way you desire right now?
Deeply in love -- Wise -- Fearing God -- Servant -- Bringing Him Glory
Choose and re-read the study from that particular day. Using the questions asked in that lesson, create your own calendar of application for the next month. Each day should have one thing "to do" to grow in your chosen area of being marked by God.
2) Commit to discovering your spiritual gifts--tests are offered online or you can read a book and ask those closest to you for affirmation. Then journal at least 10 different ways you could dream about using those to build up the body of Christ and change this world. Share with someone.
3) Decide upon 2-3 new ways you could serve your church or the defenseless in the next 2 months. Get whatever details are needed and make the commitment. Mark your calendar and follow through.

My Commitment to Grow

I, _____ have chosen one commitment from each area listed above.

I will commit to living out one growth opportunity at a time, in whatever order I choose. I am going to share this commitment and what it entails with _____. I will ask this person to keep me accountable--trusting her to be honest with me and to desire my growth as well.

I will ask her by _____ (date) and I will check in weekly with her on _____(day of week) until I have fulfilled all three of my growth commitments.

Note: Put alarms on your phone to remind you of key dates, check-ins, etc.

If needed, I know that I can seek additional prayer, encouragement, or support from _____ (an older woman).

Remember as God is transforming you into His woman...
STOP   LOOK   ASK   CHANGE

As my heart jumps up and down rejoicing on behalf of the journey you've taken with God, I couldn't leave without praying for you....

Almighty Precious God, seal the work You have done in my sister's heart. Protect it. Guard it. May the truths that You have planted only grow deeper from here, and may they bear much fruit for Your glory. I beg on my sister's behalf, may she spend the rest of her life as a confident, free woman leaving Your mark on every person she encounters. May she hunger to look in Your Mirror of Truth, always be willing to ask herself the hard questions, and then have the courage to live out whatever You reveal to her. May she fall in love with You more and more deeply as each day passes. Amen.

Believing in you,

Christie Lee Rayburn

For weekly encouragement, sign up at my website @ ChristieLeeRayburn.com To share with me how God met you in this study, email me @ mirror-mirror@ msn.com

To be encouraged through blogs, follow @ ChristieLeeRabyurn.com/blog

Soon-To-Be-Released **Mirror of Truth** Videos that can be downloaded to accompany this study @ ChristieLeeRayburn.com

Printed in the United States
By Bookmasters